Nicaragua is hurting.
Nicaragua is wounded.
Nicaragua is bleeding.
There is much work to do,
and there will be more work to do
because the church is divided.
Only God can save us and lead us out of this situation.
So I ask the Nehemiah Center
to continue their fight and not give up.

Lydia Velasquez,
Nehemiah Center Leader in
Strategy for Urban Transformation

To Be Reborn

The Nehemiah Center's Second Decade Transforming Lives and Communities

By Carol Van Klompenburg

To Be Reborn: The Nehemiah Center's Second Decade Transforming Lives and Communities.
Copyright © 2020 by the Nehemiah Center. All rights reserved. No part of this book may be used or reproduced in any manner whatsoever without written permission from the Nehemiah Center, except in the case of brief quotations embodied in critical articles or reviews.

Print ISBN: 978-1-7345829-2-5

Library of Congress Control Number: 2020910257

Published in the United States of America by the Write Place, Inc. For more information, please contact:

the Write Place, Inc.
809 W. 8th Street, Suite 2
Pella, Iowa 50219
www.thewriteplace.biz

Cover design by Stephanie Ten Hove and interior design by Alicia Hamming Navarrete, Nehemiah Center, Nicaragua.

Interior photos courtesy of the Nehemiah Center. All photos are used with permission.

The events, locales, and conversations in this book have been set down to the best of the author's ability.

View other Write Place titles at www.thewriteplace.biz.

Contents

Acknowledgments vi
Introduction vii
1. National Upheaval Amid Diminishing Funds 3
2. 2010–2015: The Lean Years Begin 13
3. Strengthening Managua Churches 25
4. ACECEN Grows Up 39
5. Learning to Run Businesses and Manage Money 51
6. Building Friendships Across Continents 63
7. Shifting to Urban Development 81
8. The Nehemiah Center Responds to the 2018 Crisis 93
9. Planning for the Future 103
Appendix A 114
Appendix B 115
Appendix C 116
Appendix D 117
Appendix E 118
About the Author 119

Acknowledgments

A heartfelt thank-you to the following for assistance in the creation of *To Be Reborn*:

- Alicia Hamming Navarrete, who thought of this project, walked alongside me through the entire process of interviewing, writing, and fact-checking, and then did the layout.
- Stephanie Ten Hove, for taking staff photographs and designing the covers.
- The Nehemiah Center communications staff, for providing photographs.
- The national and international collaborators of the Nehemiah Center, who graciously provided time and information whenever I requested it.
- The members of my Pella Writing Group whose chapter-by-chapter suggestions and feedback strengthened the narrative. You know who you are.
- Honey Estrada, for doing the interviews for some of the "Meet the Team" sidebars.
- Anne Petrie, for her meticulous proofreading of the manuscript.

Carol Van Klompenburg

Introduction

As I began to gather information about the Nehemiah Center's second decade for a sequel to *On Mended Wings*, a long-time Nehemiah Center collaborator warned me, "Carol, if your first book about the Nehemiah Center were a blockbuster movie, this sequel would be a box-office flop."

I was shocked, but I soldiered on. I talked with Alicia Hamming Navarrete, the Nehemiah Center's coordinator for this second volume. To refresh her memory, she reread *On Mended Wings*. While reading it, she told me, "Carol, every time I review a chapter of that first book I think, *Everything has changed*!"

I was surprised, but as I gathered the information for a book about the second decade of the Nehemiah Center, I began to understand what both of these people had told me.

Staff members sometimes wryly referred to parts of that first decade of the Nehemiah Center as "fat cow" years, thinking of Joseph in Egypt and his vision of the coming years of plenty. By inference, they saw the second decade as the "lean cow" years.

Even during those "lean cow" years in Egypt, however, God provided. Joseph's brothers emigrated from Canaan to Egypt and survived those seven years of famine. God was faithful.

As I researched the story of the Nehemiah Center 2009–2019, I learned that Alicia was right: the center had changed—immensely. And that long-time collaborator was also right: this second decade would not make a sweetness-and-light, feel-good movie.

If mended wings had been the image for the Nehemiah Center's first decade, I gradually concluded that rebirth was an apt image for its second ten years.

Over the centuries Nicaraguans have experienced hardship in many forms: natural disasters, war, injustice, and poverty. But they have been resilient. They have found ways to survive, and then to be reborn.

Perhaps the story of the Nehemiah Center's second decade is the history of Nicaragua in miniature. There have been setbacks and hardships, but, like the Nicaraguan people, the center has been graced with resilience. Its mission of transforming lives of Nicaraguans and North Americans continues. Perhaps, like a butterfly in a chrysalis, it is on the verge of emerging. With faith and hope, it is moving forward—*To Be Reborn*.

Carol Van Klompenburg
Spring 2020

To Be Reborn

The Nehemiah Center's Second Decade Transforming Lives and Communities

By Carol Van Klompenburg

Masaya Volcano, one of eight active volcanoes in Nicaragua

01

National Upheaval Amid Diminishing Funds

On April 18, 2018, Nicaragua exploded with unrest and violence. Nicaraguans—both students and the population at large—went to the streets in protest against the government. They demanded the withdrawal of a series of changes to the social security system—increasing social security taxes and lowering benefits—that had been meant to save the system from bankruptcy. The result was at least forty-nine people dead, more than one hundred wounded, and an unknown number of people missing. Mediation and government repeal of social security changes were not enough to appease the protesters.

In succeeding days Nicaragua was plunged into a severe crisis. Protests and roadblocks on almost every major highway made travel difficult. Crime ran rampant, and people were afraid to leave home after dark. Giant metal tree sculptures—a project of Rosario Murillo, wife of President Daniel Ortega—were toppled. Government and police buildings were burned. TV news channels were taken off the air.

Business activity and commerce plummeted. New shopping malls stood empty. Many jobs were lost, and many jobless Nicaraguans left the country to seek employment elsewhere. Direct foreign investment and tourism decreased dramatically. Nicaragua's Central Bank reported losing US$563.5 million in cash deposits,[1] and the government withdrew from the Central Bank more than US$107 million to offset plunging tax revenue. Some economists estimate that the economy was set back seven to ten years.

People felt a sense of deep loss. Violence escalated in almost every city in the country, and the death toll rose to 215, according to reports from national human rights organizations. The Nicaraguan government saw the violence as an attempted coup.

---

1. With the sudden surge of job losses, people didn't have the money to deposit in their bank accounts. Furthermore, people were uncertain how banks would react to the crisis, and there was fear that banks would become unstable. So people stopped making deposits.

International organizations began assisting with negotiations. Those organizations included the Inter-American Commission on Human Rights, the Office of the United Nations High Commissioner for Human Rights, the Organization of American States, and the European Union. However, the negotiations produced few results.

Evangelical churches remained on the periphery of the conflict. Congregations were deeply divided, with some members favoring the demonstrators and others favoring the Nicaraguan government.

Shoes On and Ready: A Teen Responds to the 2018 Crisis

During the uncertainty of the 2018 national crisis, seventeen-year-old Derek looked out the window of his home in León and saw the people swarming the streets outside, pointing their guns into his family's gated patio. Alarmed, he quickly alerted his family. His mother and sisters quickly closed the windows and fearfully peeped through the cracks while his baby brother slept. Derek's father had just gone out to visit someone.

"Derek, what are you doing? Don't you even think about going outside now!" his mother hissed at him in a low voice as she heard him putting on shoes in his room. She texted her husband, "Don't come home until I tell you. The street is full of people with guns."

The family watched as the men peered at the church and the parsonage behind the church, guns pointed and ready.

The family's hearts pounded with fear. They wondered what would happen if the men decided to jump the bars in front of their home and confront them. They heard shouts as the men called to each other, signaling and watching some unknown threat.

The family remembered recent nights when people had burned the nearby police station. They thought of the mob that had threatened to burn the house of a neighbor for sheltering a paramilitary sharpshooter. The neighbor had angrily retorted that the mob would need to burn the church as well, because the police had gone through church grounds as well. The mob eventually calmed down and dispersed.

Derek's sister remembered her classmate who was gunned down in the street while walking to a neighborhood store to purchase a snack. He was found dead, with seventeen bullet holes in his body. Derek's mother and her teenage children discussed what they would say, what they would do, and how they would keep the sleeping child in the bedroom safe if the people decided to enter their property.

After about an hour, the armed men dispersed. When the danger had passed, and an "all clear" message had been texted to their father, the family members waited for him to return.

Then Derek's mother asked him, "What got into you? Why did you put on your shoes?"

He answered, "Mom, if the men decided to take me away, what could you have done to stop them?" He had put on his shoes to be ready for capture.

If Derek was taken, he didn't want to leave with bare feet.

The Nehemiah Center felt the impact, seeing its income for the last half of 2018 shrink by US$36,000—due to the cancellation of all team visits from North America. In August, the center needed to cancel contracts of four administrative staff members and reduced all other administrative staff from full-time to 80 percent time.

In a letter to constituents, Director Luz Lopez requested prayer for staff members without work, for families who had lost sons and daughters to armed violence, for renewed hope in the midst of crisis, and for supporters to help lift the center from its financial crisis. Comparing their situation to that of Old Testament Israel in Egypt, she asked for prayers "that we can catch a glimpse of the good and spacious land that God has promised to us."

Group photo of Nehemiah Center staff, 2018

In a subsequent newsletter, Hultner Estrada, who was appointed Nehemiah Center director in July 2018, wrote, "The year 2018 will be difficult to forget because, among other things, all of a sudden we as Nicaraguans had to walk through the darkest valley."

That darkest valley followed on the heels of several already stressful years for the Nehemiah Center.

Years of Austerity Measures

Back in 2015, several collaborators had ended their partnership with the center,[2] and its collaborating agencies began to have fewer discretionary funds.

Looking back on these shifts, Joel Huyser, global area director for Latin America and Asia with Resonate Global Mission, said, "In its initial years the Nehemiah Center was, for the most part, funded by the mission agencies that started it. But today people like to give directly to causes

---

2. Five collaborating agencies remain associated with the Nehemiah Center: EduDeo, Missionary Ventures International, Partners Worldwide, Resonate Global Mission, and World Renew.

Meet the Team: Bridging Two Cultures

Alicia Hamming Navarrete, Nehemiah Center Communications Coordinator

Alicia Hamming Navarrete first came from Canada to Nicaragua in 2007 as a short-term volunteer for Worldwide Christian Schools (now EduDeo). She worked in Nicaragua Christian Academy (NCA) Nejapa, which had just opened on the Nehemiah Center campus. She already knew she was wired to help people. "The Nehemiah Center staff talked with us about walking alongside people long-term and developing agents of change—and it struck a chord with me."

She added, "I was attracted to the center's holistic way of doing ministry—collaborating in making resources come together—with a biblical worldview that all things belong to God. That was already ingrained in me, and it was exciting to see it lived out in a new way."

She knew already during that first visit that she wanted to return to Nicaragua. After deliberating, praying, and consulting with friends, she did—as a ten-month volunteer to coordinate semester-abroad programs for college students. "I grew to love what I was doing. There was no turning back." Alicia decided to become a Resonate Global Mission partner missionary. She traveled back to Canada and began finding donors to partner with her. She was blessed not only with funding, but also with affirmation. "People said, 'We knew this was going to happen, Alicia. We are not surprised. We are so glad you have found a place that you love.'"

With funding in place, in 2008 she continued developing the Nehemiah Center's semester-abroad programs for students from the United States and Canada. "There was still more work to do, developing that program," Alicia said. "I had just scraped the surface. Continuing the work was a natural step." Alicia also began helping coordinate other teams from North America.

Then, her life began filling up. In 2011 she met and married Maynor Navarrete. A year later their son, Myles, was born. And the workload kept growing. In 2014, Alicia decided it was time for a year off.

When she was ready to return to work, the semester-abroad program was on hold—but the center needed a communications coordinator. Alicia said yes. "It seemed like a really good change for me. It was a new focus. I could stay at my desk, have regular office hours, and spend time with my son. In addition, communications still fit with my vision of my personal mission as a bridge between two cultures."

Alicia wanted to add to her skill set for the position, so she set out to either master the skills she needed or find assistants with the needed skills. She studied social media and created strategies for communicating with her North American audience. Alicia found a professional editor with available volunteer hours and also brought a graphic design intern on board. She worked on establishing Friends of the Nehemiah Center as a US-based nonprofit for donations from US residents.

Alicia said she has learned over the years that mission work is not just about going to a different country. "Missions is a way of life and the way you obey what God has called you to. Everyone is a missionary; I just happen to be doing that in Nicaragua."

Alicia and Maynor now have two children, and Maynor is working on his permanent Canadian residency. In the future, Alicia may be doing her mission work in Canada. However, even from Canada, Alicia plans to keep working as communications coordinator for the Nehemiah Center. That bond, she already knows, can span continents.

---

they support and might even distrust larger institutions like those that founded the Nehemiah Center. One unfortunate consequence is that these agencies often have less discretionary funding available to give to ministries like the Nehemiah Center."

He added, "This trend is not unique to Nicaragua or to the Nehemiah Center. It is global."

In 2016, the Semester Program in Nicaragua (SPIN) program was canceled due to low enrollment and lack of a coordinator. SPIN had brought six to eight Dordt College[3] students to the Nehemiah Center to study Spanish, along with Nicaraguan history and culture, biblical worldview, and community development. Since 2008, each SPIN had provided the Nehemiah Center with about US$20,000 in revenue. SPIN was again on the agenda for 2018, but then was canceled because of the unrest and potential lack of safety for the students.

Luz Lopez, who was the Nehemiah Center's director from 2015 to 2018, remembered, "It was like the perfect storm. And it was caused by things outside of our control." Despite decreasing income, the center was able to balance its budget by reducing administrative costs and increasing its income from housing and feeding teams.

In the Nehemiah Center newsletter at the end of 2016, Luz wrote, "For the last sixteen years, I have worked at the Nehemiah Center, and this is the first time that I have had to completely place my trust in God's abundant grace in such a vulnerable way."

She added, "It has not been easy: we have encountered big challenges, we have traversed new roads, and when we have come to detours, we have not given up. Through it all God has shown us a new way to reach our destination."

She described the center's prudent and creative stewardship, its work clarifying and

---

3. A Christian liberal arts college in Iowa, Dordt College became Dordt University in 2019.

restructuring programs, and its daily renewal of hope in God's strength.

As part of the restructuring, the Service and Learning Institute was eliminated. Previously, this institute had a broad umbrella of responsibilities including the SPIN program, as well as short-term service-and-learning teams, student internships, college interim programs, long-term volunteers, and more. Alicia Hamming Navarrete, coordinator for the institute at that time, said, "It got really big with a lot of initiatives and volunteers. Its structure was ambiguous, with a result of uncertainty and confusion." When funding shrank, some institute staff were released, and the work of the institute was absorbed by the collaborating agencies. Each agency became responsible for hosting and organizing its own teams. The Nehemiah Center charged the agencies fees for housing teams in its dormitory and for providing them with meals.

The wide hallways of the Nehemiah Center, an invitation for collaboration

No longer needed to supervise the institute, Alicia was eventually assigned a different role: communications. As she began updating the Nehemiah Center website, she realized it had no mechanism for receiving donations. In its early years, with agency support, this mechanism had not been needed. Now, with donors more interested in direct connections, a donation mechanism was more important. She soon discovered that donating to the Nehemiah Center was a complex process for North Americans. "There was no way to make direct donations to the center," said Alicia. "There were only convoluted processes, channeling the funding through other organizations."

Ten years earlier, Nehemiah Center staff had attempted to set up a United States nonprofit support agency, but couldn't find the necessary board members. Alicia decided to try again. "I said that perhaps we could find five board members. We prayed about it, explored the options, and developed a proposal which was approved by the Nehemiah Center board in 2016."

This time people from across the United States consented to appointments to a board for Friends of the Nehemiah Center. As a 501(c)(3), Friends of the Nehemiah Center was eligible to receive tax-deductible donations from US citizens. In June 2017, a five-member board, with Gordon Tans as president, held its first meeting, online via Skype.[4] The board began increasing the Nehemiah Center's visibility in the United States and soliciting donations for the center's work.[5] In its first year of operation it received more than US$30,000 in donations. By mid-2019 those donations totaled US$105,000.

In addition, as the Nehemiah Center's financial support from international agencies diminished, it increased its collaboration with individual churches. The three church friendships covered in Chapter 6 have been part of this shift, along with support from congregations such as Immanuel Christian Reformed Church in Fort Collins, Colorado; Bethel Christian Reformed Church in Listowel, Ontario; and Guelph Christian Reformed Church in Guelph, Ontario.

Stringency measures continued to be effective through 2017. Then came the sociopolitical upheaval of April 2018. By August 2018, most of the violence and protests had subsided into an uneasy truce. According to government estimates, about two hundred people died. Other estimates claim four hundred total deaths. Road barricades disappeared, and residents could travel to get groceries and gas. Local tourism slowly resumed. But the events from April through July had devastating long-term effects. Some people had aided the protestors. Others had opposed them. There was a lot of distrust between neighbors.

During the crisis, many of the center's usual programs had been suspended. The Strategy for Urban Transformation was suspended in León and Chinandega, as well as the Church Strengthening Program in Managua.[6] León, always a politically passionate city, was especially paralyzed. Surrounded by barricaded streets, residents could not leave their homes.

The pastors also wondered how to preach God's Word to divided congregations. Finding answers was not easy. Words such as "peace" and "justice" became high-risk because of specific political connotations. So did phrases like "in solidarity," "love Nicaragua," and "seek dialogue." One pastor said, "As I went up on stage [in church], I was trembling with fear, asking God not to let any word escape from my mouth that could be wrongly interpreted."

Their congregations were not only traumatized by the crisis, but also became extremely polarized—and the polarization grew to the level of hatred, marked by moments of open confrontation. People were expected to choose a side. If pastors decided to take intermediary positions, they might be seen as cowards or traitors.

---

4. In 2019, Friends of the Nehemiah Center board members were Hannah Buteyn, Lora Kleinsasser, Gordon Tans, Marlo Van Klompenburg, Jennifer Van Zante, and Rachel Ver Meer.
5. Donations to the Friends of the Nehemiah Center can be made online at https://www.friends-nc.org. Or checks can be mailed to an address listed on that website.
6. Urban Transformation is covered in detail in Chapter 7; Church Strengthening is in Chapter 3.

"I have a sense that there are people monitoring what we are saying from the pulpit," said one pastor, clearly terrified. "Really, we only want to say to everyone to keep praying, nothing else. If we say something more, it could be used against us."

Andy Baker, who had just begun working with the Church Strengthening Programs in 2017, said, "The Nehemiah Center concluded that the current Church Strengthening Programs were no longer relevant in the new reality. Pastors didn't want to learn about healthy churches, but about how to get their people through tomorrow."

The Nehemiah Center needed to change the focus for its third decade of work. To understand the Nehemiah Center's 2018 response to the Nicaraguan crisis, it is important first to review its work in the previous decade.

Meet the Finance Team: Keeping Track of the Numbers

Karina Espinoza Ruiz, Hilda Solis, and Victor Jimenez

Three people keep track of the finances of the Nehemiah Center. Head Accountant Karina Espinoza Ruiz, age thirty-eight, has worked for the center since 2003. Victor Jimenez joined the center in 2013, and Hilda Solis began in 2014. Both Victor and Hilda work as Karina's accounting assistants.

When Karina finished college, she began working for Christian Friends of Latin America, a prison ministry that rented space at the Nehemiah Center. When that organization left Nicaragua, she began to work for the Nehemiah Center instead. Looking back over her years on the Nehemiah Center campus, she said, "I have grown during my years here—in my work experience and in interpersonal relationships. I have also grown spiritually through the workshops and devotional times provided here."

Karina Espinoza Ruiz

Karina said she likes learning from the day-to-day experiences of her job. "I have learned to fix mistakes, and I look for ways to do things better, following the recommendations of our audits and conforming to the changing laws for our work."

Her goals include improving professionally, purchasing a personal vehicle, and starting a family. When not at work, she enjoys spending time with her husband and friends, reading self-help books, and spending time in nature.

Victor, thirty-two years old, was recruited to the Nehemiah Center by its former head accountant, Juan Granados. Victor described his colleagues as "warm and sweet." He explained, "People don't gossip or speak badly of each other. They are concerned about others—promoting love, comradeship, and unity." He said he enjoys analyzing problems and finding solutions for them, and he likes to be productive.

He said that as a single person, he dreams of someday owning a house and having his own car. "I know these wishes can't be met in a short time, but with patience and the help of God, one day they will become a reality." When he is not working, he enjoys spending time with friends and seeing movies—both action movies such as *The Avengers* and romances like *Maid in Manhattan*. In November 2019, Victor resigned from his position and moved to Spain for more opportunities.

Victor Jimenez

Hilda, age twenty-seven, said she especially likes doing bank reconciliations—making sure that the Nehemiah Center's numbers match those of the bank. Her least favorite job is filling in at the reception desk and not knowing the answers to people's questions about food and lodging. She likes to work fast, but said she also has to work carefully. "In accounting there should be no errors!"

One of her goals is to learn English, and she sometimes watches movies in English with Spanish subtitles. She likes a range of movie genres, including action, comedy, and romance. Hilda is single and lives with her mother not far from the Nehemiah Center.

Hilda Solis

On the rooftop of the Cathedral in León, Nicaragua

02

2010–2015: The Lean Years Begin

The Nehemiah Center was launched in 1999 as an interdenominational ministry to respond to the devastation that followed Hurricane Mitch. In October 1998, Hurricane Mitch had blown into Central America. A Category 5 hurricane, Mitch devastated Nicaragua. In some parts of the country, 127 centimeters of rain fell, generating landslides that buried entire villages. Virtually all of Nicaragua experienced flooding. Thousands lost their lives. Hundreds of thousands were homeless. Roads and bridges collapsed, crops were destroyed, and animals died. Water was contaminated, and both food and water were in short supply. After Hurricane Mitch, the people of Nicaragua not only needed emergency relief; they also needed to rebuild their society's infrastructure.

In the wake of catastrophe, the Nehemiah Center offered Nicaraguans a biblical worldview—a belief in a God who loves not just His church, but His entire creation. Following a vision conference, the center offered a series of workshops, to build not just healthy churches but also robust businesses, schools, and families. Some believe the Nehemiah Center's best work in its first decade was in assisting pastors and church members to build healthy family relationships.[1] The center focused much of its work in the cities of Chinandega and León.

In 2010, the Nehemiah Center entered a second decade of working with Chinandega and León churches. In its new five-year plan (2010–2015), the center included continuing to strengthen these churches and schools with workshops on education, family and marriage, and church health. The center also planned to assist members of the churches of León and Chinandega to become agents of urban transformation in their communities. A third part of the plan was to launch biblical worldview training in Estelí, 150 kilometers north of Managua, a prominent stop on the Pan-American Highway with a temperate climate and a population of 119,000.

---

1. The story of the birth and first decade of the Nehemiah Center's life is recorded in Carol Van Klompenburg with Donna Biddle, *On Mended Wings: Transforming Lives and Communities in Nicaragua* (Pella, IA: The Write Place, 2011).

However, the plan ran into difficulties. "By August 2013 there was a growing sense that something was out of whack," said Steve Holtrop, long-term missionary in Nicaragua for Resonate Global Mission. The work with León and Chinandega churches was ending, but that phaseout was difficult because it was more than just a program—it had become a set of deep relationships. Furthermore, an assessment of the new urban transformation programs in those cities revealed little statistical data that showed impact.

In addition, the structure of the Nehemiah Center itself was beginning to shift. In 2009, the core of the center was formed by nine collaborating international agencies, essential to its work.

> **Meet the Team:** God Opens and Closes Doors
> *Steve Holtrop, Regional Missional Leader for Central America with Resonate Global Mission*
>
>
>
> In 1997, after graduating from Calvin College, Steve Holtrop worked alongside a church planter in Puerto Rico for six weeks. There he learned he could survive—and even thrive—in another culture. He returned to the United States with a new career goal. Instead of being a civil engineer, he wanted to do mission work in another country.
>
> While still a college student, Steve had felt nudged toward international mission work, but he had decided it would be wise to complete his civil engineering degree first. After completing that degree, he took the prerequisites for entering Calvin Seminary and enrolled there to study for a master's degree in missions and church growth. When he completed that course work, he worked construction jobs in Michigan while his wife Kim completed her master's degree in social work.
>
> In 2001 Steve and Kim moved to Haiti—a two-year commitment for Steve to work there for Christian Reformed World Missions.[1] Kim worked in denominational women's ministries. "Haiti was a transformative education," Steve said. "We knew no one. We spoke little Creole."
>
> He ran headlong into the risks of creating dependency. "We were surrounded by Haitian pastors and leaders who were looking to us for answers. I thought, *Why are you looking to me for direction?* But they waited to hear what I would say, and then they would agree with me. They would build on my ideas because I was a source of funding. That funding provided them with financial security, so they were making a totally understandable choice."
>
> As those two years came to an end and there was no longer work for him in Haiti,

---

1. Later renamed Resonate Global Mission.

he and Kim considered work in several locations—one of them the Nehemiah Center in Nicaragua.

"We really liked the idea of the Nehemiah Center—a place where Resonate and World Renew and other organizations worked together," Steve said. That collaboration had initially drawn Steve and Kim to Haiti as well.

When they visited Nicaragua, Joel Huyser, one of the Nehemiah Center's founders, took them directly to the home of a Nicaraguan church leader. Steve remembered, "When we got there, he had ordered pizza. He had taken the liberty and personal initiative to show us that hospitality. Haitians would have expected the North Americans to provide the pizza. I appreciated his initiative."

Steve added, "Then the Nicaraguan leaders shared information about their ministries with us. If we wanted to be part of these, that would be great. They showed us a level of independence that was encouraging to us."

In addition, the Holtrops already had a bond with one of the North American families working at the Nehemiah Center: Mark and Nancy Vanderwees. "Everything fell into place," Steve said. "We have learned over the years that God opens and closes doors for us. We never have to force them. At least that is how it has worked for us."

The Holtrops made an initial five-year commitment. "In order to build relationships, local people need to know that you will be with them long-term," Steve said.

That five-year commitment ended in 2008, but in 2019 Steve and Kim were still working in Nicaragua. "Why would we leave?" Steve asked. "My call to work in Nicaragua continues to be confirmed."

Over the years, Steve's roles and responsibilities for Resonate Global Mission have changed. But whatever his assignment, he has been known at the Nehemiah Center as a person who remains calm during conflict. He can maintain a peaceful relationship with people who disagree with each other and can help them to work together toward a common goal.

He said that requires a flexible communication style. "With a Canadian I might be a bit more blunt. Talking with a Central American I need to be a bit more vague and fuzzy—to be blunt would be offensive. But if I am vague with North Americans, their response might be a blank stare. I need to understand both styles and both points of view."

Has living in Nicaragua changed him? He paused, reflected, and said, "I suspect it has."

He chuckled and added, "It has made me a little more tan. And I've had to master Spanish." (Ironically, one of his reasons for his civil engineering major had been to avoid a foreign language requirement.) "It has made me more patient with others—although my kids probably wouldn't agree with that!" Steve and Kim have four children.

Steve reflected a bit more and added, "I never really was a black-and-white thinker, but now I am even less so. There are so many factors in so many situations that it is very difficult to make rules about things. I have come to value clarifying conversations. I definitely value different cultural perspectives more than before. And I have learned that I am part of an incredibly privileged minority in terms of wealth. It has been an amazing privilege to live outside of my home culture and to learn from that."

16   To Be Reborn

In 2011, Food for the Hungry, which had been a collaborating agency, appointed a new country director. Under new direction, the agency's collaborative vision faded. It switched to simply renting office space at the Nehemiah Center and pursuing a separate course of action. Also in the second decade, several other collaborators changed their focus to other Central American countries and to other Nicaraguan ministries. Caribbean Ministries Association, for example, began refocusing its work by launching youth ministries in Cuba. Missionary Ventures International began to put more energy into creating satellite schools, similar to Nicaragua Christian Academy Nejapa.²

Leaders unified with the heart of God

Running parallel with this shift was a new life-stage for the Nehemiah Center as an institution. The normal early institutional stages of high energy and loose structure were strained. Collaborators felt a need to have relationships, accountability, and structure more formally defined. This loss of initial momentum and need for more structure are typical of the second stage in the life cycle of institutions.³

In the wake of the 2007–2009 recession, charitable giving declined, and the funding of the center's collaborators declined along with it. As funding shrank, the collaborating institutions put more restrictions on their donations to the center. "In the early years, the donations went into one pot, but that was no longer the case," said Steve Holtrop. "Those early years were an anomaly." This increasing "silo effect" was part of a global funding pattern. NGOs locked their donations into a specific purpose with defined parameters. While this accountability had benefits, it also limited local initiative and creative freedom.

For a variety of reasons, the center's biblical worldview training had less success in Estelí than similar programs in Chinandega and León. The program began in Estelí with one hundred people attending a four-day vision conference. A series of monthly workshops followed, but the number of people attending dwindled. Program funding also decreased. "When we began the

---

2. Nicaragua Christian Academy International, a K-12 school in Managua, was begun in 1991 as a Christian school in English for children of missionaries to Nicaragua. Nicaraguan children soon began attending also. In 2013 and 2015, NCA launched additional schools, with instruction in Spanish. For more information, see https://nca.edu.ni.
3. P. D. Masterson and C. T. Thompson, "Life Cycle of an Organization" (2007), https://www.snpo.org/resources/documents/LifeCycleofanOrganization.pdf.

> **Meet the Team:** Keeping the Center Looking Good
>
> *Juan Sevilla, Grounds and Maintenance*
>
>
>
> Since 2008, Juan Sevilla has been the person in charge of maintaining the Nehemiah Center buildings and grounds. He makes repairs, paints buildings, waters flowers, and trims trees—whatever is necessary to keep the center looking good and running smoothly. Over the years, he has witnessed the construction of new buildings and the planting of new trees.
>
> Juan dreams of building a canal on the campus to control water during the rainy season, but said he would need additional help in order to accomplish that.
>
> Juan lives just three blocks from the center, where he grows corn and beans in his personal garden plot. One of his goals is to save enough money to buy more land for his gardening.
>
> Juan likes the majority of his maintenance tasks, especially taking care of the trees and watching them flourish. He dislikes work that requires him to climb atop a roof. He explained, "I feel insecure and am afraid that I will fall!"
>
> He described himself as both easygoing and easy to get along with. When not working, he enjoys watching television and listening to Christian reggae music.
>
> Juan and his wife, Jessica, married when he was eighteen years old. They have two children.

program in Estelí, we had US$35,000 per year for the program. In the last year, we had only US$15,000," said Luz Lopez, who was then one of the three trainers for the Estelí program.

Biblical worldview workshops had already been taught to Estelí educators and parents by ACECEN,[4] an organization of Nicaraguan Christian schools. In addition, Estelí, as a more prosperous tourist center, had been influenced by a prosperity gospel, making servant leadership somewhat less attractive to them. There were fewer local champions for a biblical worldview in Estelí than in cities where the Nehemiah Center had previously worked. In addition, Estelí's distance from Managua and its higher cost of living made it a more expensive location for the staff to travel to, eat in, and find lodging in. The twice-a-month trek and training eventually became exhausting for the three trainers.

---

4. Acronym for *Asociación de Centros Educativos Cristianos Evangélicos de Nicaragua* (Association of Centers of Evangelical Christian Education of Nicaragua).

> **Biblical Worldview in Brief**
>
> Either consciously or subconsciously, each human being has a worldview, a basic way of knowing, which includes all of that person's knowledge. A person's worldview answers six fundamental questions: What exists? Where does it all come from? Where are we going? What is good and what is evil? How should we act? What is true and what is false?
>
> A biblical worldview answers these questions with the grand story of creation, fall, redemption, and consummation:
>
> **God created the world good.** People lived in harmony with God, with others, with themselves, and with the rest of creation.
>
> **We rebelled against and disobeyed God and evil entered the world.** When evil entered the world, all four relationships were damaged.
>
> **God sent His Son Jesus to the world to begin to make the world good again,** to restore fractured relationships. Christians are called to be His hands and feet in shaping and reshaping the world in keeping with God's desire for its healing and wholeness. A biblical worldview, then, includes not only the traditional elements of worship (prayer, Bible reading, and singing praise to God) but also all of the activities of daily life. Especially important in the biblical worldview at the Nehemiah Center is the understanding that the world, though it is fractured and broken, still belongs to God. So Nehemiah Center staff work to bring wholeness in education, business, finances, marriages, etc.
>
> **Jesus is returning to earth at the end of time, when God will again make all things perfect.** Meanwhile, we work day by day toward that wholeness and healing which God will perfect at the end of time.

By 2014, facing internal and external challenges, collaborators appointed a team of key players and board members to evaluate the Nehemiah Center's status and create a new five-year plan. This team gathered information, prayed, reflected, and planned. Out of their work rose a new vision. The previous vision had broadly included "individuals, churches, organizations, and local communities," and a mission to weave together agents of transformation into "local, vocational, and global networks of learning, service, and collaboration." The revised vision focused on collaborating with churches to strengthen them in their mission in God's world. Included in that vision was continuing to build cross-cultural relationships between Nicaraguan and North American churches for their mutual transformation.

According to the plan, the work of strengthening churches would switch from Estelí to Managua, where the Nehemiah Center was located. Word of the center's good work in León and Chinandega had sparked interest among Managua churches. This focus would reduce travel costs, and allow better use of the Nehemiah Center facilities as a location for the workshops for Managua churches. Working in Managua, the country's capital city with a population of approximately two million people, also fit with the need for programs matching the global trend toward urbanization.⁵ Improvements in the cultural center of the country could eventually impact other parts of the country. Urban missions expert Ray Bakke explained, "Cities function as magnets and magnifiers of culture. On one hand, cities import the nations; this is the magnetic pull-factor. On the other hand, cities also export culture; this is the magnifying push-factor."⁶

Daniel Boniche passes on the baton to Luz Lopez as the new director of the Nehemiah Center.

Expanding on these push-pull factors, Street Psalms Senior Fellow Joel Van Dyke said, "The city is a magnet that draws people seeking opportunity and fleeing oppression. As such, it gathers and compresses humanity's greatest hopes and its greatest fears. The compression transforms them into noble gifts as well as unspeakable curses."⁷

At the same time as it shifted to a local focus, the center streamlined its operations to reduce costs. When Daniel Boniche and Juan Granados retired as executive director and office manager/director, their work was combined into one position and filled by Luz Lopez, a long-term Nehemiah Center staff member and trainer.

"Many of us had wondered if the Nehemiah Center was going to fold," remembered Steve Holtrop. "Then, in July 2015, we started to feel as if we had turned a corner. Both the Ezra team [Nicaraguan nationals] and internationals were energized by the idea of focusing on strengthening churches in Managua. We were excited that a vision had been clarified, and team members felt a sense of ownership."

---

5. According to the United Nations, about 55 percent of the world's population lived in cities in 2018. That 2018 study predicted that this percentage would rise to 70 percent by 2050. A European commission had higher estimates. Using high-resolution satellite images to determine the number of people living in a given area, the commission concluded that 84 percent of the world's population already live in urban areas.
http://theminnesotasun.com/2018/07/13/researchers-everything-weve-heard-about-global-urbanization-turns-out-to-be-wrong.
6. Quoted in Kris Rocke and Joel Van Dyke, *Incarnational Training Framework: A Training Guide for Developing Incarnational Leaders Engaged in City Transformation* (Street Psalms Press, 2017), 21. Street Psalms is a global network that develops incarnational leaders—leaders who embody the presence of Christ in hard places.
7. Rocke and Van Dyke, *Incarnational*, 25.

Meet the Administrative Team: They Keep the Center Running Smoothly
Leonor, Christina, and Cindy

Three women administer the day-to-day operations of the Nehemiah Center. Together they have worked for the center a total of thirty-nine years. All three are married, are in their mid-life years, and have young children at home. And together they keep the Nehemiah Center running smoothly.

- Leonor Vasquez works as the receptionist and oversees the logistics of the facility and its guesthouse, booking room rentals and food for events on campus.
- Christina Solis reports to Leonor and makes sure that the guesthouse is ready for occupants and that cleaning and meals take place as scheduled.
- Cindy Huerta is an assistant to the Nehemiah Center director and to the Ezra team (the Nehemiah Center teachers). She also supervises security and maintenance personnel as well as information technology.

Christina and Cindy grew up in Nicaragua, and Leonor is from the neighboring country of El Salvador. All three women said they enjoy working for the Nehemiah Center. Leonor likes the friendly atmosphere and the fact that each day her work has different tasks. Christina is grateful for the support she received from colleagues following her surgery and after the death of her mother. Cindy appreciates the many things she has learned while working for the center. Her work has stretched her. She said, "In spite of my fear of doing new things, I say yes to new assignments because I am working for God."

Leonor added that she has learned that Christianity isn't just going to church. "It is more than that. It is my communion with God every day, and it is in my relationships with my mother, my friends, and my neighbors."

At home, Christina enjoys cooking, and as supervisor of food at the center, she dreams of someday expanding its kitchen area. Cindy said she enjoys serving others and accomplishing tasks on time.

Some of this energy rose out of a weekend spiritual retreat in which team members examined their own spiritual health. Some of it came from reading *Center Church* together, available in both Spanish and English. In that landmark book, Tim Keller offers a vision for renewal, church planting, and church ministry in the city. And some of it came from participating in Synergy, a conference held in nearby Guatemala that focused on how to transform and develop cities.

"In the fall of 2015, we had a special assembly of the board of directors," Steve Holtrop said. "They approved the new Five-Year Strategic Plan. We felt a new identity and sense of belonging. We had a sense of purpose instead of a sense of aimlessness. This shift was also true for donors. They had something to hold on to."

Meet the Team: Sharing Lives—and Work
Luz Lopez, Nehemiah Center Executive Director 2015–2018, and Manuel Largaespada, Teacher and Coordinator

Luz Lopez and Manuel Largaespada married in 1987, and both of them have been part of the Nehemiah Center ever since it was launched following a 1999 conference for Nicaraguan pastors. Luz assisted with housing and food arrangements for the conference. Manuel worked for Food for the Hungry, one of the three organizations sponsoring the conference, so he helped to organize the conference as well.

In 2001, Luz accepted a job teaching the Nehemiah Center's marriage workshops. Manuel joined her in this teaching—as a volunteer. That pattern has continued for them: often one of them has worked as a paid staff person for the center, and the other has come alongside as a volunteer.

In those early years Luz did more than teach marriage workshops. When the commercially available manual was deemed too expensive, she created a curriculum for that course. Her curriculum worked well. When a manual for business training was needed, Luz was asked to work alongside a business expert and write that training manual. A second business manual, on developing a business plan, followed.

Over the years Luz and Manuel were part of expanding the family training to include minimizing domestic violence and preventing AIDS. Manuel spent several years working for the Nicaraguan Bible League, but continued to assist Luz whenever she taught marriage classes.

Luz assisted with the research into a church strengthening curriculum, and eventually became supervisor of the Ezra team—the Nicaraguans who taught the Nehemiah Center's courses.

Early in 2015, Luz requested a leave of absence. She needed time to recover from several taxing years both professionally and personally. The Estelí teaching workload had been demanding, and she was grieving the deaths of three of her siblings. She was also caring for her father following his cancer diagnosis.

She returned to the Nehemiah Center in October 2015 when the center's board of directors asked her to become the center's executive director. With her gentle voice and calm demeanor, she was a stabilizing force amid diminishing funds and rapid change. She also systematically streamlined and pared down the center's processes. Facing recurring health challenges, she resigned from that position in August 2018.

After the 2018 sociopolitical crisis, Manuel returned to work for the Nehemiah Center facilitating pastor roundtable discussions. Luz began assisting him with those roundtables as a volunteer.

Asked whether they talked about their Nehemiah Center work in their evenings at home, Luz chuckled and said, "Of course!" She added that they also talked about books they were reading, about the Bible, and about theology. "Manuel likes to discuss what he wants to preach and teach. He loves those topics," she said.

Luz and Manuel have two adult sons who live abroad, one in the United States and the other in Taiwan.

Pastors and church leaders gather together in the Nehemiah Center *ranchón* for worship during a Vision Conference.

03

Strengthening Managua Churches

As part of its 2015 five-year plan, the Nehemiah Center combined several programs into one and called it *Departamento de Fortalecimiento Eclesial* (Church Strengthening Program). To find churches for this program in Managua, the Nicaraguan capital city in which the center is located, staff members used existing links and relationships. ACECEN, the association of Christian schools that had been launched by the center, had connections with Managua churches that sponsored Christian schools. The center staff had connections with additional Managua congregations, especially those in Nejapa, the *barrio* (neighborhood) surrounding the center. Staff members created a map that included all neighborhood congregations and went church to church, inviting leaders of each of these churches to a vision conference entitled "For Jesus and the City."

On May 25, 2016, fifty-two church leaders gathered at the Nehemiah Center *ranchón*, a spacious open-air gathering space with a thatched roof, to learn about the new Church Strengthening Program. The program would have two phases. In the eleven weekly sessions of Phase 1, the churches would learn about a biblical worldview and then assess their congregation's strengths and weaknesses. In Phase 2, they would be able to choose from several options, deciding which would be most helpful for their congregation.

Better Churches Phase 1

Thirty-eight church leaders enrolled in the first phase of the training. Because of classroom space limitations at the center, half the group met each Friday and half each Saturday. They used materials from *Red de Multiplicación* (Multiplication Network),[1] a program created by Dr. Juan Wagenveld, based on his experience planting a church in Puerto Rico. Since 2007, Multiplication Network has been widely used to strengthen churches in South and Central America.

---

1. More information available at http://www.reddemultiplicacion.com. Used by permission.

26 To Be Reborn

As Managua's church leaders used Multiplication Network tools to take the pulse of their congregations, they learned about the five vital elements and five vital functions of a healthy church.[2]

A healthy church has the following vital elements:
- A clear and inspired vision
- A leadership that inspires and multiplies, that has character and vision, and that influences its members
- A congregation that is the body of Christ, with all of its members motivated to serve
- Good stewardship of all resources
- Biblical text conveyed appropriately in the context of the community

---

[2]. The Nehemiah Center adapted these tools to fit the Nicaraguan context and the center's dialogue-based education format.

> **Meet the Team:** Helping the Church Become a Community of Servants
> *Hultner Estrada, Nehemiah Center Executive Director*
>
>
>
> Hultner Estrada, who became director of the Nehemiah Center in June 2018, grew up as the son of a well-known Nicaraguan pastor, a leader in his denomination whose voice was heard across the country on both Christian and secular radio stations. As a teen, Hultner accompanied his father to his weekly broadcasts and learned firsthand how radio stations work. In college he majored in journalism. At age twenty-five, Hultner became manager of a major Christian radio station in Nicaragua and, like his father, he also became a well-known radio voice across Central America.
>
> Then he met Manuel Largaespada, accepted a job working alongside Manuel at the Nicaraguan Bible League, and watched Manuel lead Bible League devotions. Hultner remembered, "It was very different for me because he did not preach or teach. He used dialogue. It was my very first experience of dialogue-based Bible reflection. I was impacted by his method of leading these devotions."
>
> He also came to know Manuel's wife Luz Lopez, who worked at the Nehemiah Center. "When I met Luz and Manuel, I felt something out of my known world," he said. "I came from a very Pentecostal background. They were different people. They were so motivated to living out the gospel in a holistic way. They encouraged pastors to live out Bible principles for their marriages and finances and politics. It was fantastic to see. It touched my heart."

When Hultner had met Manuel and Luz, he had told them his goal. "'I want to be the person who will gain more souls per minute than anyone else in this nation. I will win more souls than any other person in Nicaragua.'" He added, "I had a very spiritual focus."

Knowing Hultner's media background, Luz asked him to help create video testimonies for the course she was teaching to pastoral couples. In June 2005, when starting a program that included arts, media, and youth, the Nehemiah Center appointed Hultner as its facilitator. It was a good fit. In addition to his radio station experience, Hultner had worked as a youth pastor in his father's congregation.

In his early years at the center, Hultner worked in all three areas, but eventually recognized that this scope was too broad. He began to focus on the youth program, using material from Street Psalms. He and his team worked with more than a hundred churches and pastors in four Nicaraguan cities: Chinandega, León, Estelí, and Managua. Central to the Street Psalms teaching was incarnational living—learning to be the presence of Christ amid the least, the last, and the lost.

In 2013, while studying the Faithwalking series,[1] Hultner experienced a fresh encounter with Jesus. "I realized that my behaviors—my preaching, leading Bible studies, presenting the gospel—had been learned as the son of a pastor. They came from my mind instead of my heart."

He told a pastor friend, "I need to accept Jesus as my Lord again."

Hultner remembered, "He anointed me with oil, I cried a lot, and I encountered Jesus. After being a Christian for more than thirty years, I accepted Jesus as my Lord again."

Growing out of that experience was a new goal for his life. "I want to help the evangelical church become the loving and active body of Christ again—to be a community that serves others instead of being an institution composed of conquerors."

In 2015, when Luz became Nehemiah Center director, she suggested that Hultner replace her as the manager of the Ezra team, the center's team of Nicaraguan teachers and trainers. And in 2018 when Luz left the director position, the Nehemiah Center board selected Hultner as its new director.

Hultner is fluent in English and a proficient pianist, having studied music at a conservatory for two years. He also enjoys cooking, which he learned at home as the oldest of four children. His parents taught him that he was responsible for helping his younger siblings, as they were both committed to co-pastoring their congregation. Hultner says his best dish is garlic shrimp. He uses the small shrimp caught and sold at local markets, not the shrimp grown on Nicaraguan shrimp farms for export. "The shrimp I use are smaller than the farmed shrimp," he said. "But I think they have better flavor."

Hultner's wife Tania volunteers at the Nehemiah Center, helping with clerical work and running errands. Hultner and Tania married in 1999 and have two children: a daughter, Honey, and a son, Esteban.

---

1. https://www.faithwalking.us

They learned that an unhealthy church has the opposite qualities. The vision is unclear and or not inspired. The leadership does not permit change and multiplication. Only some of the congregation are motivated to serve. Not all resources are used fully and faithfully. And the preaching of the biblical text is unbalanced—focusing too much on either the text or on the context.

Attendees also learned the following vital functions of a healthy church:
- Evangelism (in word and deed)
- Training disciples
- Holistic and compassionate service
- Communion and fellowship
- Worship (balanced, biblical, inspiring, and involving)

Pastors receive training in Better Church workshops at the Nehemiah Center.

In contrast, an unhealthy church practices one-sided evangelism—either word or deed, but not both. It only maintains believers instead of training disciples. It serves only individual spiritual needs and uses few resources to cultivate a united church body. Its worship is not balanced, makes minimal use of the Bible, and inspires only a few members.

Participants also learned that overall, a healthy church is growing inwardly (in communion, relationships, and discipleship), outwardly (in service, evangelism, and witness), and upward (in adoration of God).

The Nehemiah Center staff assisted the churches in their self-evaluation, as they looked at their biblical focus, their mission, and the needs of their neighborhoods. The training sessions included worship, reflection, and planning.

The goal of gathering information was to improve functioning churches, and it was not intended for churches that were experiencing significant strife and antagonism. Each church conducted a survey of as many members as possible, including the church leaders. They tabulated the leader surveys separately from the general membership to see if the responses of the two groups were similar.

"In the beginning we were afraid of how the congregations would react to the surveys," said Pastor José Daniel Borge, pastor of *Príncipe de Paz* (Prince of Peace), "but after the first work session, all of the leaders were very enthusiastic about the process and were motivated to continue."

> **Transformation Story:** Pastor Sanchez and Villa Venezuela
>
>
>
> Villa Venezuela is one of the most dangerous neighborhoods in Managua, Nicaragua's capital city. *Nueva Jerusalén* (New Jerusalem) church is located in Villa Venezuela. Describing it, Pastor Harold Sanchez said, "Here there are a lot of drugs, many unemployed youth, and lots of robberies and delinquency." Despite the dangers, he continues to preach the gospel, and church members are dedicated to their troubled neighbors.
>
> As part of this dedication, the congregation wanted to become a healthier church. Early in 2018, Pastor Sanchez and two church leaders traveled twenty kilometers through congested Managua streets to participate in Better Church workshops at the Nehemiah Center.
>
> Pastor Sanchez said the workshop's list of indicators of a healthy church opened his eyes to new places to direct the congregation's attention. He called the workshops a blessing and said they had been filled with interesting information.
>
> Using the materials from the Nehemiah Center, he multiplied the impact of what he learned by sharing lessons about indicators of a healthy church with the twelve members of New Jerusalem's leadership team.
>
> When the Nehemiah Center made a follow-up visit to the congregation, they saw that church leaders were fostering a much clearer vision to impact their troubled community. They had developed stronger leadership and a larger commitment to disciple the marginalized people surrounding them.

At the conclusion of Phase 1, church leaders responded appreciatively when asked about their best memory from the past six months. "My best memory is of the fellowship that we enjoyed with other ministries in the city," said Miguel Cubillo, pastor of *Asambleas de Dios* (Assemblies of God) church.

Edwin Gutiérrez, a leader at Prince of Peace church, commented, "For me, the best part was participating in the health diagnosis for our church and realizing the elements and vital functions that we need to strengthen."

Better Churches Phase 2

Based on the survey results, each congregation's church leaders created an action plan for their congregation. To help the implement this plan, they chose two courses from the Phase 2 training options, taught by Nehemiah Center staff. These options included:

- A Timothy Leadership Training for pastors, taught by the late Henry Cruz
- A marriage and family course, Restoring the Original Model for Marriage, taught by Luz Lopez and Manuel Largaespada

Transformation Story: Gilberto and Nuria

Thirty years after their wedding, Gilberto and Nuria thought they had a solid marriage. Nevertheless, when the Family Counseling course was offered as part of the Nehemiah Center workshops for strengthening churches, they signed up. The course inspired them to take a second look at their relationship, and they realized they had some unhealthy behavior patterns—patterns they had accepted from their families of origin and their culture. Nuria commented, "When our economic situation became tense, Gilberto got uptight." Verbal fights followed. They agreed that during the counseling course they learned to speak to each other with respect, even during moments of strong disagreement.

They said that by taking the course they also learned to rest—to know that God wants them to trust Him with their burdens and to take time for relaxation and recreation. Gilberto said it was a challenge for him to realize that their three adult daughters have lives of their own, and that he and Nuria can go out without taking the entire family. Nuria commented, "Now we define times to go out together. We seek out recreation and enjoy the moment—eating chicken, going to visit family in a cooler part of Nicaragua, or just people-watching."

They enjoy dedicating time to each other as a couple. During one class, when asked about their goal as a couple, Gilberto joked, "Not to die right now!" He wanted more days and years to spend with Nuria.

When the class stopped chuckling, Gilberto listed other goals such as improving daily in his service to the Lord and the church. Gilberto and Nuria are associate pastors of *Centro de Fe y Vida Nueva* (Center of Faith and New Life) in Managua.

Nuria added that they also dream of a better home and owning a truck, but she agreed with Gilberto that their priority is to see families in the congregation working in the church and serving God.

- A Street Psalms incarnational ministry course on reaching the least, the last, and the lost ones, taught by Hultner Estrada
- A Planting Healthy Churches course, taught by Henry Cruz

Sixty-three people from thirty different congregations attended the Phase 2 training, which ran from January to November 2017.

Henry Cruz facilitates a workshop at the Nehemiah Center.

Pastoral training course

The pastoral training course enhanced the skills of church leaders, using materials developed by the Timothy Leadership Training Institute (TLTI). TLTI was created in the 1990s in response to the rapid growth of the Christian church in the developing world, led by pastors with minimal training for their roles as pastors and church leaders.[3] Timothy Leadership Training has since been implemented in more than forty countries and thirty languages.

The Managua pastors' leadership skills were strengthened by six training modules in the following topics:

- Biblical preaching
- Pastoral care
- Stewardship
- Combating domestic violence
- Praising God in work and worship
- Christian education/God's plan for sustainable development

At the beginning of each lesson except the first, all participants presented reports of what was accomplished since the last lesson. Together they reflected on and discussed Bible passages, asking questions and discerning principles. They learned to listen carefully and express their ideas clearly. Each participant wrote a plan to put into practice what was learned and then

---

3. In 2019, the Timothy Leadership Training Institute became part of a new ministry of leadership resources called Raise Up Global Ministries. More information about the Timothy Leadership Training program can be found at https://www.raiseupglobal.org/leadership/tlt. Used by permission.

reported on implementing that plan at the next meeting. At the end of each class, participants prayed, committing their plans to God.

Pastor Manuel Hernandez, from *Misión Príncipe de Paz* (Prince of Peace Mission) church, summed up his experience, saying, "Here I learned that I continue to be a disciple of Jesus, and I need to keep learning about Christ to gain a vision for our ministry."

Sergio Gallegos, pastor of the *Monte Fresco* (Cool Mountain) Church of God in Managua who had taken the course a few years earlier, commented, "Among the errors that one commits in preaching is to not prepare well beforehand. We have had the habit of reading the selected Bible passage, and then just standing in front of the congregation and saying some things here and there about it. The Timothy Leadership Training Institute helped us see these as errors, even though we thought they weren't that big of a deal. But they are big errors! We are responsible for the 'flock' that God has given us, and we have to give them the good food of the Word of God."

Marriage and family counseling course

Luz Lopez, a Nicaraguan psychologist who was a long-term staff person at the Nehemiah Center, created the marriage and family counseling course. She had co-taught the course with her husband Manuel many times. The course's focus was to repair what was broken in the relationships of pastoral couples. "Hurt people hurt people, and healed people heal people," said Luz.

When teaching the course, Luz and Manuel used Luke 12:39 as a motto: "But understand this: If the owner of the house had known at what hour the thief was coming, he would not have let his house be broken into."

"Marriage and family are sensitive subjects," said Manuel. He added that it causes him some fear each time he addresses the subject with pastoral couples. The verse implies a warning that produces discomfort: care for your home because someone has plans to plunder it.

"It is a call to action," he said.

Luz added, "Nicaraguan pastors know a lot about how to take care of their homes in the spiritual sense, but they need to grow in their understanding of the importance of other areas, such as the emotional and physical health of their homes."

The course included the following content:
- Modifying patterns of living and practicing good treatment of one's spouse as a lifestyle. This includes respecting a spouse's opinions, tastes, and customs; listening; and stating one's opinion without shouting or treating one's spouse poorly.
- Recognizing that God wants us to have good health and to be attentive to our habits of exercise and healthy eating.

- Making the decision to reduce some heavy and unnecessary yokes that produce exhaustion in the pastoral family. These yokes include self-image, legalism, and overcommitment.
- Breaking the code of silence regarding a poor relationship or spousal abuse.

Luz Lopez facilitates a marriage and family counseling course for pastoral couples.

Josefa Vargas and the late Marcos Vargas, pastors of *Iglesia Peniel*[4] (Peniel Church) and professors at Nicaraguan Bible Seminary, expressed gratitude to God for being able to participate in the ten sessions of the marriage and family counseling course. Marcos said, "Pastors need to be pastored, and in the marriage and family counseling course we felt pastored. We found what is oftentimes difficult to find in other places."

"We felt pastored; we received fellowship, advice, and confidence," added Josefa.

Incarnational ministry course

The incarnational ministry course adapted materials from Street Psalms, whose goal is to train the heads, hearts, and hands of urban leaders to love their city and seek its peace.[5] The course was originally created for ministry with urban youth, and the Nehemiah Center used it for that purpose in its first decade. In its second decade the center adapted the material for broader use—with urban church ministries for people of all ages. The course emphasized working with marginalized people who are outside the church. It explored six dimensions of this work:

- The Word made flesh: Jesus was born from below. This dimension's missional question was, "What is my image of Jesus, and how does it shape the way I serve?"
- In—but not of—the world: understanding the grammar of God. This dimension's missional questions were, "What changes do our ministries need to make to serve those around us? How do we love the lost without losing our purity as the body of Christ?"
- The scandal of God: loving the least, last, and lost. This dimension's missional question was, "How do we speak of God in the midst of suffering?"

---

4. Peniel (Face of God) is the name Jacob gave to the place where he wrestled with God (Genesis 32:30).
5. More information can be found at: https://streetpsalms.org. Used by permission.

- Image is everything: finding God's breath in man's dust—how Jesus calls us to see and experience the world in ways that offer authentic hope and real alternatives to those who are hopeless. This dimension's missional question was, "What does it mean to bear the image of God, and how does that call forth a ministry of imagination?"

In 2017, 75 pastors graduated from the Better Churches Phase 2 course.

- It's a family affair: redeeming our inheritance—the complex world of the family and what it means for mission in the urban context. This dimension's missional question was, "What does it mean for the church to be the family of God in contexts where families are bruised and broken?"
- City of joy: welcome to God's playground—God's heart for the city and how to live, laugh, and love in hard places. This dimension's missional question was, "How does the New Jerusalem of our faith impact the way we live and serve in Babylon?"

Church planting course

The *Más Iglesias* (More Churches) course consisted of seven workshops taught from January to July 2017 by Henry Cruz. About thirty-five pastors and leaders attended, representing twenty churches in Managua. The focus of the course was on planting new congregations that would utilize the vital purposes and functions of the church laid out in the Better Churches Phase 1 courses. The material used was developed by *Red de Multiplicación* (Multiplication Network) and adapted by Henry Cruz. Most participating churches sent their senior pastor and a leader who they envisioned could plant a church in the future. Workshops focused on:
- Evangelism
- Small groups and discipleship
- Inductive method of Bible study
- Vital functions and elements of a church
- Family
- Holistic ministry
- Spiritual disciplines[6]

---
6. Resources for this course can be found at https://www.reddemultiplicacion.com/nuestro-material/materiales Used by permission.

At the end of the course, participants were challenged to develop a plan based on everything they learned from the course. These plans were substantial documents of ten pages or more. In these documents the participants not only stated what they had learned, but also how they were already putting their learning into practice and how they planned to use their learning in the future.

Courses Completed

In November 2017 the second-phase courses were completed, and the church leaders gathered to worship and to celebrate that accomplishment. The Nehemiah Center's next goal for these churches was to train them for holistic ministry to their communities—healing their neighborhoods. Alicia Hamming Navarrete, communications coordinator for the Nehemiah Center, explained, "The goal is not just to have a healthier church, but also that the church then reach out to its neighborhood as salt and light." In 2017, the Nehemiah Center's two programs for strengthening churches' holistic ministry were *Estrategia de Transformación Urbana* (Strategy for Urban Transformation) and IMPACT Clubs.[7]

Early in 2018 the Nehemiah Center sponsored a second vision conference to launch the Church Strengthening Program with a new group of churches. The center also launched a series of roundtable meetings in which pastors discussed ministry to their Managua neighborhoods and prayed for the city. But these new programs ground to a halt in April with a political crisis throughout the country. Equipping the previously trained Managua churches for holistic mission in their neighborhoods was also put on hold.

---

7. Both programs are covered in more detail in Chapter 7.

Meet the Team: A Church Friendship and a Move Abroad
Andy Baker, International Collaborator,
Nehemiah Center Church Strengthening Program

After his first trip to Nicaragua as part of a church friendship program, Andy returned to Iowa with a passion to learn Spanish. "All I remembered from my high school Spanish was *'Hola'* (hello) and *'¿Dónde está el baño?'* (Where is the bathroom?). I told myself, 'If I want a relationship with Nicaraguans, I am going to have to learn Spanish if it kills me—and for a while I thought it was going to.'" But he persevered, using online programs such as Duolingo.

On their second trip to Nicaragua in 2016, Andy and his wife, Andrea, learned about Nicaragua Christian Academy International (NCA)—an English-speaking school where the children of many missionaries to Nicaragua are enrolled. Looking online, Andrea discovered NCA had an opening for a math teacher. Since her college years, she had felt a call to teach in a missionary school. She applied and was offered a contract.

Andy checked into openings at the Nehemiah Center and realized he could fill a need for a volunteer coordinator and international collaborator for the Church Strengthening Program. Andy and Andrea raised their support under the umbrella of Resourcing Christian Education International, with Andrea as the primary missionary.

They arrived in Nicaragua in the summer of 2017, and they were just getting accustomed to the language and the culture when the sociopolitical crisis of April 2018 began.

NCA switched to teaching classes online for the final four weeks of the semester. Many days, with roadblocks and recommended curfews in Managua, the Bakers were unable to leave their home. When they did go out, they occasionally faced lengthy waits at the grocery store.

Some of the barricades were created by protesters, and some by opportunists who charged money to those who wanted to pass. "It was frightening to face a man with a mask and a homemade rocket launcher," said Andy.

Andy and his wife Andrea, along with their two children, returned to the United States for the summer, something the family had previously planned to do. But with an uncertain future for Nicaragua, Andrea accepted a teaching job in Andy's hometown of Sioux City, Iowa, for the 2018–2019 school year and remained in the United States with the children. In late July, Andy returned to work in Nicaragua, making trips to see his family in Iowa every few months. In the summer of 2019, the Baker family was reunited. Andrea was once again teaching at Nicaragua Christian Academy International, and Andy continued to serve at the Nehemiah Center.

A child washing her hands at school

04
ACECEN Grows Up

Compared to other Central American countries, Nicaragua has the lowest primary school enrollment rate and highest dropout rate. Among those countries, it also has the highest percentage of primary-school-aged children not attending school at all. And teachers in many Nicaraguan schools lack important teaching skills.[1]

Already in 2000, the Nehemiah Center recognized the importance of improving the country's educational system and began training Nicaraguan Christian school teachers in biblical worldview and crucial teaching skills. In 2004 it launched ACECEN (*Asociación de Centros Educativos Cristianos Evangélicos de Nicaragua*—Association of Evangelical Christian Schools of Nicaragua) with twenty-three member schools.

In 2007, the Nehemiah Center began receiving funding from the United States Agency for International Development (USAID) *Excelencia* program for improvements in Nicaraguan private schools. ACECEN membership grew to more than a hundred schools. Despite the program's stellar results, USAID ended all Nicaraguan school funding after eighteen months. The teacher trainers continued their work for a time without pay. Then EduDeo, a Canada-based organization that partners with Christian schools in developing countries, began to help fund the trainers. EduDeo, formerly part of Worldwide Christian Schools, had already been helping Nicaraguan Christian schools with con-

Teachers from Belén Baptist School in Managua

---

1. https://edudeo.com/get-inspired/countries/nicaragua.

> **Transformation Story:** From Frustration to Life with a Purpose
> *Pablo Melendez, ACECEN Coordinator*
>
> It was never Pablo Melendez's dream to work with schools. He wanted to be a lawyer, earn as much money as possible, and make a name for himself. In 2000, he became a lawyer, but he was frustrated when he didn't achieve riches and fame. He remembered, "That frustration led to an empty and senseless life."
>
>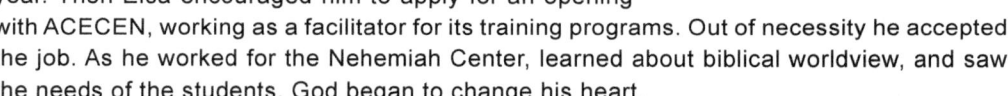
>
> His wife, Elsa, taught in a local Christian school. Their different goals and careers created distance in their relationship. Although Pablo didn't know it, Elsa began to pray that Pablo would someday work in Christian education.
>
> In 2007, Pablo lost his job and was unemployed for a year. Then Elsa encouraged him to apply for an opening with ACECEN, working as a facilitator for its training programs. Out of necessity he accepted the job. As he worked for the Nehemiah Center, learned about biblical worldview, and saw the needs of the students, God began to change his heart.
>
> He saw how teachers worked a second job in order to keep teaching Christian school students. He saw crowded classrooms and a shortage of books and supplies. He heard about broken family relationships and students coming to school hungry.
>
> "Seeing the difficult circumstances of the children awoke in me a desire to do something significant for these Christian schools," he said. "God became real in my life and my desire changed from wanting to become famous, with a heart focused on material things, to a desire to serve Jesus Christ through the gifts and talents He had given me." His work was no longer just his job; it became his passion. Pablo is now passionate about influencing the educational system so students can have a better future.
>
> In 2010, Pablo was appointed director of ACECEN. He commented, "I am very grateful to God, the people, and the organizations that have accompanied me throughout these years and have been an influence in my life. I am no longer frustrated and empty, but I have a purpose in living for Christ."

struction projects since 1999.[2]

EduDeo is closely tied to the Nehemiah Center. As a Canadian organization without legal rights in Nicaragua, EduDeo relies on the Nehemiah Center for all in-country financial transac-

---

[2]. In the early years the organization name was Worldwide Christian Schools, with offices in both the United States and Canada. The two organizations are now independent. Worldwide Christian Schools is based in the United States, and EduDeo is based in Canada.

tions. EduDeo shares Nehemiah Center office space with ACECEN. The two organizations use the offices vacated by Food for the Hungry in 2015.

In the years after its founding, ACECEN gradually worked toward independence from the Nehemiah Center, establishing its own budget, administration, board, and staff. It became officially independent of the center in 2008. Alicia Hamming Navarrete, communications coordinator for the Nehemiah Center, commented, "ACECEN is a star program of sorts because it has been so successful over the years. Birthing a separate organization was our goal from the beginning, and our relationship with ACECEN remains very strong."

ACECEN annually evaluates each Christian school that is a member of the association.

ACECEN works to train teachers in a biblical worldview and to improve the quality of Nicaraguan Christian education. "We train teachers and principals in Christian schools as agents of transformation," said Pablo Melendez, ACECEN executive director since 2010. In addition, the administrators have learned to collaborate with other Christian schools instead of regarding them as competitors, allowing for better relationships among schools.

ACECEN has eight facilitators who work with principals of member schools to improve programs, curriculum, buildings, and administration. Pablo said that before ACECEN training, teachers viewed their role as transmitting information to students. In the course of their training they begin to view their role as much broader: they grow closer to their students' lives and learn how to instill in them a biblical worldview. Pablo said, "We have seen that a biblical worldview allows teachers to see how important they are in impacting students' lives."

Teachers inspire students to make a difference in their communities after graduation. Following the creation of ACECEN's strategic plan for 2015–2019, Nicaraguan evaluation teams traveled to schools to help them understand their strengths and weaknesses. Based on the team's report, each school created an action plan to strengthen its education programs. "This process permits schools to clearly understand what they need to do in order to keep improving," said Pablo.

In 2018 and 2019, ACECEN's focus for training was restorative practices. These practices strengthened relationships and also addressed conflict and tension to repair past hurts, helping to restore a peaceful environment. One technique in this process was using affective statements and questions: What happened? Who is being affected? What can we do to solve this problem? EduDeo's Nilda Navarrete explained, "It is a way to give opportunity to the victim and the person who caused a problem to express their feelings without being judged."

ACECEN facilitators receive training from EduDeo's Walking Together facilitators.

ACECEN also distributed Gideon Bibles to 954 teachers and 26,000 students. These Bibles have been used as part of the classroom teaching.

Another dimension of the ACECEN program is building cross-cultural relationships between Nicaraguan and Canadian schools. In the "Write 2 Hope" program, fifth-grade students

Meet the Team: A Bridge for People with Passion
Lesther Gonzalez, Construction and Logistics Manager for EduDeo Ministries

Lesther Gonzalez, a bilingual Nicaraguan, acts as a bridge between his country and North America, coordinating an average of five to eight school construction projects each year. Schools that are members of ACECEN, a Nicaraguan association of Christian schools, submit construction proposals to EduDeo Ministries. Once EduDeo has approved a project, Lesther goes to the job site with local engineer Maria Boniche, who then creates blueprints for the construction.

Lesther buys the needed materials, transfers them to the job site, and then coordinates the work of a team of Canadian or United States volunteers who spend ten days launching the project. When the team leaves, he coordinates the completion of the project by Nicaraguan builders. Lesther said he enjoys it when some Canadian team members return a year or two later and he can show them the project—completed and in use.

He was nine when his parents fled Nicaragua to the United States to escape the civil war that engulfed Nicaragua in the 1980s. He lived in San Francisco, California, for twenty years, where he learned to speak English fluently. After the Nicaraguan civil war ended in 1990, Lesther often traveled back and forth between Nicaragua and the United States with his father, who earned money transporting buses and cars from the United States to Nicaragua. "Nicaragua was beautiful and fun," said Lesther. "It was special even though I had a life in San Francisco." It also felt like home, but he didn't know what kind of work he might do if he stayed in Nicaragua.

During a 2006 visit, a woman who worked for his Nicaraguan grandmother told him, "Lesther, you speak perfect English. I could get you a job here."

"Doing what?" Lesther asked.

"Translating!" she said.

That suggestion led to a job for Lesther at Global International Ministries. In 2009, he began adding part-time translation jobs for Worldwide Christian Schools. Soon he began working full-time for EduDeo.[1]

He said, "I believe that the Lord put me in this work. I meet such wonderful, good-hearted people, and I love that about my job. I meet people with passion to work for the Lord. I know that they could go anywhere else in the world seeing beautiful places, but they are here getting dirty and working hard for Him."

As a child in Nicaragua, Lesther attended Catholic mass with his parents, but when they moved to the United States they all began attending an evangelical church. Lesther continues to worship with an evangelical congregation in Managua, *Verbo* (The Word). Describing Verbo worship style, he chuckled and said, "Our worship is loud, but it is nice!"

Lesther and his wife, Zoila, have a son, Carlos, age fifteen, and a daughter, Isabela, age six. On weekends, Lesther and his family enjoy going to the Pacific Ocean, about an hour from Managua. "My daughter loves the ocean. She loves to play in the sand and the water. I like watching her from a hammock."

---

1. EduDeo was previously known as Worldwide Christian Schools Canada.

from Immanuel Christian School in Lethbridge, Alberta, co-wrote a story with students from *Primer Templo Bíblico* (First Bible Temple) School in Managua. Canadian students began the story and sent it to the Nicaraguan students, who added to it. Then it was sent back to the Canadian students, then back to Nicaragua—until the story was complete. The next step for the manuscript was printing and placement in the school libraries. The printed copy listed all students from both schools as authors and included information about both Christian schools. The story features José, who lives in San Pedro, Nicaragua, and Danielle, from Coal Valley, Alberta, who makes a trip to Nicaragua.

44 To Be Reborn

Additional cross-cultural relationships have developed through a school-to-school program. Each year a team from Gateway Christian School, Red Deer, Alberta, visits *Colegio Bautista Libertad* (Liberty Baptist School) in Managua, and a team from Abbotsford Christian School in British Columbia visits *Centro de Fe* (Faith Center) school, also in Managua.

The students in the teams are twelfth-graders, and the team size has ranged from twelve to forty-seven people who visit for ten days. During the visit, Nicaraguan and Canadian students spend time together in class, play sports activities, work on a service project, and go on a few outings. Trips have included a pineapple farm, bird sanctuary, museum, cathedral, water park, and zoo. Together, the high-school students lead activities for younger students and create photo books with English and Spanish captions. The Canadians also visit the homes of the Nicaraguan students.

Gateway School's Vice-Principal Chris Kooman said, "Students love the time that they spend with Bautista students. This is the heart of, and the highlight of, the trip. It is amazing to see how

---

Meet the Team: What You Do for the Least of These. . .
Peter and Trudy Kuipers, Volunteers with EduDeo Ministries

Peter and Trudy Kuipers of Lacombe, Alberta, have volunteered for EduDeo Ministries since 2010—the year that they sold their business.[1] In 2010, Peter was just fifty-three years old. "I didn't want to retire," he said. The verse from Matthew 25, "Whatever you did for one of the least of these brothers and sisters of mine, you did for me," spoke to Peter.

He and Trudy had made several trips to Nicaragua with EduDeo, and they decided to volunteer for this Canadian nonprofit. They began spending four to six months of each year in Nicaragua. "I really enjoy volunteering in Nicaragua part-time," he said. "I appreciate Nicaraguan life. I rely a lot on Nicaraguan contractors, and I let them take the lead. I don't try to tell them how to do things." He added that as a former business owner with a take-charge personality, he needed to work at letting others take the lead. "Nery Gonzalez and Vicente Estrada, two local Nicaraguan contractors, demonstrated solid construction and organizational skills, and we relied on them extensively to complete projects."

Trudy's knowledge of Spanish has been helpful in working with teams at job sites and maintaining good interpersonal relationships. She also organized the cleaning and painting

---

1. EduDeo Ministries works in several countries in the developing world. In Nicaragua, EduDeo has offices at the Nehemiah Center, shares with it a common purpose, and uses some of its administrative services.

> of steel roofing materials for construction projects.
>
> Peter said the work in one school has been especially memorable for him. In 2014, a 150-student school, Escuela Kenneth Hanna, submitted a proposal for a library. Principal Maria Del Carmen told Peter that after EduDeo had approved the proposal and left, she ran outside the school building and yelled, "Thank you, Lord!" The following year, when the surrounding community saw that library, the enrollment increased by one hundred students.
>
> In 2015, parents asked Maria if the school would consider adding a high school to the current grade school. With EduDeo's help, the school added four classrooms and a computer lab, enabling them to start a high school. In 2019, the enrollment had increased to 518 students.
>
> In 2018, Peter and Trudy began reducing the number of months they spent in Nicaragua and gradually turning construction supervision over to Nicaraguans.

things come together, in spite of the language barrier." He said that students at the school begin to look forward to the trip in younger and younger grades, and each year the whole school gets involved in raising funds for the trip.

Peter Kuipers, who volunteers as the Nicaraguan HANDS (Helping Another Nation Develop Schools) team coordinator with EduDeo, said, "It is a wonderful experience for high-school students to learn about each other's cultures. When it is time to leave, many friendships have been formed, and many tears are shed."

Bautista Principal Hilda Rios Rios said the Nicaraguan students are encouraged to take English courses so that they can better communicate with their Canadian visitors. Several of the Bautista students who chose to take the English courses are now working as English teachers, and they return to Bautista during the Canadian student visits to serve as translators.

The Canadian students study in preparation for their trip, taking an intercultural studies course. Included in the course is information about Nicaraguan history, culture, food, and economy.

A few times each year, some Canadian teachers also travel to Nicaragua to spend time with Nicaraguan teachers in a program called Walking Together. In addition, education experts travel to Nicaragua to train ACECEN's eight education facilitators. These facilitators, in turn, pass on this expertise to the ten or fifteen schools in each of their districts.

In 2018 ACECEN led 457 workshops across Nicaragua, helping to improve the education in its hundred member schools. It is the largest single program supported by EduDeo, which has programs in multiple countries.

> **Meet the Team:** Rejoicing in Christian School Expansion
> *Nilda Navarrete, EduDeo Ministries Coordinator*
>
>
>
> As EduDeo Ministries Coordinator in Nicaragua, Nilda Navarrete enjoys seeing the results of EduDeo's building projects at the schools. She cited an example in Chinandega where six classrooms were added to a school. On a visit there, she saw not only the classrooms but also the additional students. She celebrated the school's becoming self-sustaining through its increased enrollment.
>
> Seeing the schools reach more students motivates her in her work. "More people need to know about God. If there are more children in a Christian school, we can reach more families and also create larger, more self-sustaining schools."
>
> Nilda first worked for different organizations as a translator for North American teams to Nicaragua. She translated EduDeo's Walking Together training in 2010 and eventually became EduDeo's country coordinator in 2015. EduDeo Ministries rents office space from the Nehemiah Center and is included under its legal umbrella.
>
> Nilda said she enjoys being part of the services at the center. "There are many ministries, but we all have the same purpose—to serve God and promote the gospel. We are very united, and I like the Christian environment."
>
> Nilda has been a mother to her fourteen-year-old nephew since he was a baby, and is in the process of adopting him. In 2014, when she worked at the center as a translator, she was still angry with her sister for deserting her son. Nilda said the staff's Monday morning devotions—talking about Jesus and praying for needs—helped her move toward forgiveness during that difficult time.
>
> In her free time, Nilda is learning to dance at Managua Christian Dance Academy. She said, "It relaxes me and provides a physical workout as well."

Qualifying ACECEN schools can apply to EduDeo for assistance in constructing new classrooms. In the past decade, EduDeo has completed sixty school building projects in Nicaragua as part of its HANDS program.

Canadian EduDeo teams have traveled to Nicaragua to assist Nicaraguans with the majority of these construction projects. The Nicaraguan schools contribute part of the construction costs, an amount that varies with their financial circumstances. Teams usually have about a dozen members and raise between US$7,000 and US$9,000 to fund construction. They raise an equal amount of money to fund the team's logistical and administrative costs. Work projects last about ten days and include six work days, a cultural day, an educational day in which they visit Nicaraguan schools, a Sunday in which they worship with Nicaraguan Christians, and a travel day.

"It is a core principle that a Nicaraguan contractor leads the construction, and the teams are there to help him and his employees," said Peter Kuipers, who, along with Lesther Gonzalez, coordinates many of the teams for EduDeo. "In most cases, the team does about 10 percent of the labor, and the Nicaraguans do 90 percent. Generally, a team comes at the beginning of a project—when there is the most work."

A teacher gives a lesson to her students.

Startup work includes digging and pouring foundations, washing and painting the steel for the roof structure, and making rebar cages for the building columns. With those three jobs, there is a range of work for team members with differing strength and skills.

Peter said that most projects have produced very good results. EduDeo requires the school property to be publicly, not privately, owned. On a few occasions, classrooms have been built for a school that closes a year or two later. With the help of ACECEN, EduDeo is working to select schools that are sustainable, with the majority of the operating costs being funded by parents. Occasionally, there are exceptions. (See story in this chapter about El Shadai.)

Nilda Navarrete, a bilingual Nicaraguan, has been EduDeo's coordinator in the country since 2015, serving as liaison, translator, and office manager.

Lesther Gonzalez, also bilingual, works alongside Nilda, helping to select construction projects and implement them. He also helps host both construction and school-to-school teams from Canada. Lesther fled Nicaragua during its civil war in the 1980s and then returned to Nicaragua around 2006. He began working for EduDeo in 2009. Peter said he relies more and more on Lesther to take the lead on building projects when Peter is in Canada. "Lesther is very good at resolving issues with workers at construction projects. When he is working with teams, he really shines," said Peter.

In 2018, when all visits to Nicaragua by North American teams were suspended, Peter thought, *There goes a lot of our funding.*

Each year in September, prior to leaving for Nicaragua, he makes a short presentation to Woodynook Christian Reformed Church, his home church near Lacombe, Alberta. The following Sunday, the church's offering normally totaled about US$7,500. Following the 2018 crisis, he appealed to the congregation for funding—to be used by Nicaraguan construction teams—and the congregational offering totaled a whopping US$31,000. "The congregation knew what was happening in Nicaragua and felt connected to it," said Peter. "They were determined to continue with the construction of schools."

Transformation Story: El Shadai: An Exception to the Rule

When EduDeo Ministries constructs classrooms, most schools are required to provide a portion of the construction costs. There are occasional exceptions. One of those exceptions has been *Centro Comunitario El Shadai* (El Shaddai Community Center).

El Shadai was built just north of El Viejo, a village that was created in 1998 when people who had lost everything during the destruction of Hurricane Mitch were relocated. In the decades that followed, El Viejo remained an extremely impoverished community with few jobs available. Its houses were rusted sheets of corrugated metal with black plastic roofing. Many residents could not afford shoes.

In 2007, Juanita Paniagua Medrano, a twenty-five-year-old Nicaraguan dentist, came to El Viejo to promote the use of dental hygiene products. She began to love the people of El Viejo and felt called to launch a Christian school there. With financial help from nonprofit groups in the United States and South Korea, she purchased a property, built a school, and became its principal. A Washington, DC, foundation agreed to fund the school's operating expenses in the amount of US$940 per month for eighteen years, with a goal that the school would be sustainable thereafter. The Nicaraguan government provided rice and beans for the school's feeding program; students' parents became school cooks.

The students attended free of charge. Juanita supplemented her income by working as a dentist on weekends.

In 2013 EduDeo staff visited the school to consider a request for 200 desks. Peter Kuipers remembered, "I was accustomed to seeing poverty in Nicaragua, but this was at an entirely different level." The 225 students, preschool through grade six, sat on the concrete floors. Many of the children appeared malnourished. A few of them sat on lawn chairs, and some used pizza boxes as makeshift desktops.

Water was carried into the school in buckets, and a bathroom sewer line was plugged. EduDeo approved the funds for two hundred desks and for completing the half-finished water system. Peter said, "There was a lot of excitement when the new desks arrived. A woman from my home church had provided funds for treats for the students. This caused even more excitement."

In 2013 EduDeo team members suggested that Juanita begin charging tuition. Juanita agreed. Following a meeting with families, parents began paying five córdobas tuition per month (US$0.20) per student. By 2019 that tuition payment had grown to sixty córdobas (US$1.85) per month.

In 2014 Juanita also began lobbying the government to help pay her teachers' salaries. After four years of dogged determination, she succeeded in obtaining salaries at a rate of 50 percent that of public school salaries, enabling her to pay a more reasonable wage to the school's staff.

In the years after its first visit in 2013, EduDeo completed additional small projects at the school: cutting holes for ventilation, painting the classrooms, reinforcing the roof structure, and replacing the roof's metal sheeting, all at no cost to the school.

By 2018, the school had grown to 275 students, and Juanita requested construction of a new preschool classroom and office. When EduDeo staff met with Juanita in 2019, they challenged her to contribute US$1,500, 10 percent of that project cost. She smiled at the staff and said, "I am so appreciative that we are now in a position to contribute."

Peter remarked, "This school has touched our hearts. It is a privilege to work alongside Juanita. She reminds me of Matthew 25:40: 'Whatever you did for one of the least of these brothers and sisters of mine, you did for me.' Juanita began this school in faith, and EduDeo's partnership with her has blessed us all."

The Good Sense curriculum teaches about financial stewardship.

05
Learning to Run Businesses and Manage Money

The lack of formal, well-paying jobs (those that offer a contract, fixed salary, benefits, and social security) has caused the majority of Nicaraguans to create their own businesses to be able to support themselves. As recently as 2016, 75 percent of employed Nicaraguans worked in this informal sector.[1]

As a result, Nicaraguan cities have a multitude of small businesses: corner convenience stores, food stands, small pharmacies, tortilla stands, bakeries, and used clothing stores. The streets are filled with vendors of juices, fruit, hammocks, car parts, and even exotic dogs. Using their cars and bicycles, Nicaraguans also offer transportation services. The country's economy and employment depend on these small businesses.

However, many of these business owners lack appropriate training. About 55 percent of small-business owners have only a primary school education or no education at all.[2]

Already in 2001, the Nehemiah Center had begun filling this knowledge gap with a Kingdom Business Program—providing technical assistance and training in biblical principles to Christians running small businesses.

The course included the following principles:
- God calls businesses and entrepreneurs to serve His kingdom.
- A business is like a mission field in which owners can share the gospel message.
- A business can serve to enrich the kingdom of God.
- God is the owner of businesses, and Christians should operate their businesses in a way that honors Him.
- A business should maintain good order—paying taxes, paying debts, and paying fair wages to employees.

---
1. https://www.thedialogue.org/blogs/2016/04/thinking-differently-about-nicaraguas-development-challenges.
2. Ibid.

The businesspeople in León and Chinandega had expected business loans to follow their training, a practice typical of non-government organizations in Nicaragua. But such loans were never part of the Nehemiah Center plan; its working model had always been to provide training, not financial aid. Friction and resentment followed this misunderstanding. As a result, by 2010 the Nehemiah Center's Kingdom Business Program was on hold.

AECNIC board members

Nevertheless, the need for training continued. In 2011 the Nehemiah Center hired Freddy Méndez to rebuild relationships with Chinandega and León businesspeople. In his previous work as a leader of CECNIC (*Comunidad de Estudiantes Cristianos de Nicaragua*—Nicaragua's InterVarsity group[3]), Freddy had been known for his coordination and relationship skills. After attending training to develop his business skills, Freddy contacted about ten businesspeople in Chinandega and León, using a list from the Nehemiah Center. As he contacted them, he also worked on healing past hurts and resolving conflicts. He listened to the businesspeople talk about their needs and how they could best be helped and mentored. They enrolled in a business course he offered to them.

After taking classes and building mutual trust, these people identified a hundred Chinandega and León business leaders to attend a planning conference in León. These leaders recommended small training workshops and identified three group purposes:

- Develop entrepreneurs, providing them with Christian principles and business tools. To accomplish this, Freddy organized a six-session business course. It included topics such as setting goals; creating a business plan; doing a SWOT analysis (Strengths, Weaknesses, Opportunities, and Threats); studying the marketplace; marketing; production process; basic accounting; and legal requirements. All of these were taught

---
3. InterVarsity is a Christian ministry on college campuses.

using biblical principles.
- Develop Christian business disciples by sharing what they had learned in their training—helping other business owners and motivating them to work together. Fatima Davila, a Chinandega businesswoman, took this challenge seriously, training five women in business skills and even helping a few of them with starter loans. Women were especially active in the program, at one point outnumbering men 65 percent to 35 percent.
- Create a network through which Christian businesspeople could gather, learn from each other, and pray for one another.

Freddy and Pablo Melendez, a Nicaraguan lawyer, also helped business owners with the necessary legal paperwork for creating a business association. Partners Worldwide began to assist in the development of these businesspeople, providing North American business affiliates as mentors and sounding boards. The international specialty of Partners Worldwide is partnering with businesses in the developing world.

"Partners Worldwide exists to build up local organizations that self-identify as the go-to resource for small business owners in their own community," said Bob Vryhof, a Partners Worldwide regional director. "To end poverty, you need a thriving business community."

Vryhof ticked off a list of key items which are less accessible for people in marginalized communities: business knowledge, a network of peers, access to funds, and advocacy.

By 2014 the León and Chinandega businesspeople decided to form their own association, a legal entity to be recognized by the Nicaraguan government. They named their group AECNIC (*Asociación de Empresarios Cristianos de Nicaragua*—Association of Christian Businesspeople of Nicaragua). Over the next two years they created an eight-person board of directors and took steps to become a government-recognized association. By 2017, the Nicaraguan government had recognized AECNIC, and its members held their first assembly as a legal Nicaraguan entity. They had achieved independence and were now ready to leave the Nehemiah Center's umbrella of care. Freddy eventually transitioned to work for the Nehemiah Center as coordinator of *Departamento de Fortalecimiento Eclesial* (Church Strengthening Department).

By the end of 2018, the twenty-four micro- and small-business owners who were AECNIC members had become very close—sharing their struggles and assisting each other in overcoming challenges. Among the subjects they had studied were how to calculate their break-even point and how to separate their business and personal finances.

AECNIC continues to have a close relationship with Partners Worldwide, which offers them education and training but does not provide loans or grants. The first students in the Partners

> ### Meet the Team: Appreciating Bonds of Confidence and Trust
> *Freddy Méndez, Church Strengthening Department*
>
>
>
> In 2011, Freddy Méndez began working for the Nehemiah Center to rebuild relationships with León and Chinandega businesspeople. When hired, he was already acquainted with the work of the center: his wife, Leonor Vasquez, had been working there since 2005.[1]
>
> Freddy coordinated the business program and taught its classes. Then the businesspeople launched their association, AECNIC, and took responsibility for their own courses and training. Freddy subsequently began working with the Nehemiah Center Church Strengthening Department. In 2019 the Church Strengthening Department included trauma healing circles, kingdom finance workshops, pastoral roundtable discussions, and pastoral retreats.
>
> Freddy said he appreciates the strong bonds among Nehemiah Center staff members. He added, "We trust each other, and therefore we have healthy relationships. I like it that we are a family."
>
> As a Christian, he also appreciates the Christian environment of the center. "My purpose is to follow Christ and relate to Him as His son. The Nehemiah Center promotes an integral gospel, imitating Jesus so that we live as God wants. That is why I feel connected with the Nehemiah Center: it aligns with my purpose."
>
> He also appreciates the bonds in his biological family. "We have a lot of trust and confidence in each other," he said. He and Leonor married in 2004 and have two children. The family enjoys traveling and eating together—especially in restaurants.
>
> What does he enjoy about his work? "That we help people to deepen their relationship with God, and we encourage them to be more like Jesus every day."
>
> His least favorite part of his job? "Sitting through long meetings."
>
> ---
>
> 1. See page 20 for information about Leonor Vasquez.

Worldwide business curriculum completed their training in June 2019. The AECNIC board alternates its monthly meetings between Chinandega and León.

From Business Skills to Personal Finances

Jesse and Jari Rodriguez first visited Nicaragua in 2016 and considered relocating to Nicaragua from their home in Grand Rapids, Michigan. Jari is a registered nurse and Jesse has a bachelor's degree in finance. Jesse said, "What drew me to Nicaragua was that there were businesses everywhere—kids selling tortillas, women selling bread from their homes. I thought that with a little more knowledge they could take their businesses to the next level."

During his visit, he learned about the need for an assistant with the Nehemiah Center's Kingdom Business Program, led by Freddy. He saw a match. "We felt God's call to come and help with the program."

In 2017 Jesse and Jari Rodriguez began assisting Freddy in training AECNIC members. Jesse met with the AECNIC board members, working with them in developing their business models. Since several of them were in health-care businesses, Jari's medical background and fluent Spanish were also useful.

Then the Rodriguez's plan turned a corner. When Jesse arrived, AECNIC had already begun transitioning from the umbrella of the Nehemiah Center. He wasn't needed for long at AECNIC. But in those first months in Nicaragua, he had seen another need. "We discovered a recurring theme," he said. "Many Nicaraguans had problems with their finances and personal budgets." A survey of six hundred Nicaraguans by Elaine Miranda, a Latin American finance blogger, had revealed that 87 percent of Nicaraguans had some form of debt and that 56 percent of them spent more than 30 percent of their income to pay off debts. Some 27 percent dedicated more than half their income toward the payment of debts.[4]

Jesse had done financial coaching in Michigan, and he recognized that Nicaraguans had the same needs for financial coaching as his former students in Michigan. He suggested that the Nehemiah Center begin a stewardship training program, exploring what God had to say about finances and money in contrast with the messages from the surrounding culture. The Nehemiah Center had been sensing the same need in pastoral families.

Jesse Rodriguez leads a Good Sense workshop.

In August 2017, the same year the Kingdom Business Program ended with the independence of AECNIC, a Kingdom Finance Program was launched. Jesse and Freddy taught a trial version of the course to the Nehemiah Center staff.

---

4. Elaine Miranda, "Los nicas y las deudas: los resultados de la encuesta," https://plataconplatica.com/los-nicas-las-deudas-los-resultados-la-encuesta, quoted in Luz Lopez, Nehemiah Center Newsletter, May 2018.

The Nehemiah Center staff then did a survey of evangelical Christians in Managua, and the survey revealed a special interest among men twenty-five to thirty-five years old, most of them single. The survey indicated they wanted to better control their finances, get out of debt, and eventually purchase a home.

In 2017 the Nicaraguan economy was booming, and young professionals had easy access to credit. They bought appliances and vehicles on credit. "In this country, in which a dollar per hour is a good salary, people had US$500 to US$700 per month car payments," said Jesse. "And

> **Meet the Team:** Hearing God's Gentle Yes
> *Jesse and Jari Rodriguez, Finance Trainers*
>
> When Jesse and Jari Rodriguez visited Nicaragua in 2016, God had already been preparing them for their ministry with the Nehemiah Center.
>
> Jesse and Jari had been living in Grand Rapids, where Jesse and Jari worked with the youth group of *Iglesia Cristiana Reformada Emanuel* (Emmanuel Christian Reformed Church)—work that Jesse gradually became convinced was not his calling. He knew God had called him to use his business expertise, but didn't understand how that fit with his work serving his Lord.
>
>
>
> Then, in 2011, Jesse became aware of the Partners Worldwide business curricula that provide a path from poverty to sustainability. He participated in a pilot class from this curriculum taught to his Spanish-speaking congregation by Renita Reed. While he was part of that course, Jesse thought, "Hey—this works!" He saw that mentoring people through this business program could be his ministry, and he became one of the first four people in the Partners Worldwide Business Affiliate Team in Grand Rapids.
>
> A few years later, Jesse met Daniel Espinosa in Grand Rapids, Michigan. Daniel was then Nicaragua country director for Partners Worldwide, and he sparked interest in serving in Nicaragua for both Jesse and Jari, who is Nicaraguan. Their church in Grand Rapids was closing, they wondered what was next for them, and they began praying about God's next calling in their lives. Then came their 2016 visit to see family members in Nicaragua.
>
> Shortly after that visit they discovered an opportunity to work in Nicaragua under Christian Reformed World Missions (now Resonate Global Mission). Despite many thoughts screaming "No!" Jesse and Jari said they heard God's gentle "yes," stronger than the screaming. They moved in October 2016 to work at the Nehemiah Center.
>
> Jari remembered, "I had feelings of excitement, and I was a little nervous about returning to Nicaragua. But, having learned about this great ministry, I was excited to see God use

Learning to Run Businesses and Manage Money

> Jesse's talents and experiences in the areas of business and finances for God's kingdom work. As for me, I knew in my heart I would be doing ministry alongside my husband. This brought me joy because we would be serving God's people!
>
> "I had questions for God: How is this going to work out, leaving our home in Michigan, fundraising, and my husband and I working in ministry together?
>
> "God reminded me of His sovereignty and promises! In the days and weeks that followed, He encouraged me through His Word that He would take care of us as His fellow workers. He would be working right alongside us and the Nicaraguan church for His purpose!"[1]
>
> How has God transformed them through this process? Jesse said, "Before, I was always hustling for money, wondering how much I could make. Then I learned about the Quadruple Bottom Line in the Partners Worldwide business curriculum."[2]
>
> He learned to consider not only economic issues, but also spiritual, social, and environmental ones. He wanted to teach other entrepreneurs what he had learned. He learned, and he teaches others, that business people can bring Christ to the world every day—just as pastors and evangelists do.
>
> ---
> 1. Bible verses that especially encouraged Jari were Matthew 6:25–26, Hebrews 13:21, and 1 Corinthians 3:9.
> 2. The Quadruple Bottom Line is a concept from Renita Reed, International Coordinator for Discipling Marketplace Leaders. See sidebar on page 61.

appliance stores made rent-to-own offers in which borrowers ended up paying three times the value of the items they bought. The young professional Christians who were deacons or who led ministries were living in debt."

He asked himself, "How can churches grow and have impact when their members are struggling with mountains of debt?"

Freddy and Jesse set a launch date and invited people to a meeting about worshiping God with finances and managing finances in a God-honoring way. They hoped for a group of forty. Fifty-two people came.

"We packed them into a conference room and explained the plan, telling them that there are 2,300 Bible verses about money," said Jesse. "Their reaction was 'Wow!'"

Jesse chose *Buen Sentido* (Good Sense) materials from Good Sense Movement as the curriculum.[5] The first course began in September 2017 with twenty-one students, and it matched the demographic that had indicated a special interest in the topic—young men who were pastors, directors of ministries, and deacons.

When beginning the course, students filled out questionnaires about how much they owed, how much they had, how much they gave away, how much they spent, and how much they earned in a year.

---
5. https://goodsensemovement.org.

They also answered questions that helped them discover the significance of money in their lives, whether they saw money as a means to liberty, to security, to power, or to love.

The Good Sense curriculum taught students five biblical characteristics of Christian stewards:

- Diligent Earners: They work with commitment, purpose, and a grateful attitude.
- Generous Givers: They give with an obedient will, a joyful attitude, and a compassionate heart.
- Wise Savers: They build, preserve, and invest with discernment.
- Cautious Debtors: They avoid entering into debt, are careful and strategic when incurring debt, and always repay debt.
- Prudent Consumers: They enjoy the fruits of their labor yet guard against materialism.[6]

Participants learn about personal finance through the Good Sense course.

In more practical terms, the course set up the following expectations for students:

- Participants will draw near to God as they learn to manage their resources as an act of worship to God.
- Participants will increase tithes and offerings to local churches.
- Participants will establish a savings account, reduce or cancel debts, and maintain a budget.
- Participants will mentor two other people within their social networks (church, family, neighbors).[7]

When the first course was completed, it was repeated for other students. At the end of 2018, thirty-one students from Managua and several surrounding *barrios* (neighborhoods) had completed the course. The goal was that they would become teachers of the course in their communities. They continued to meet in six different follow-up groups. James, a student in the first course Jesse taught, had been excited about what he was learning. But when Jesse tried to follow up with him, Jesse couldn't reach him. "I figured you can't win them all," said Jesse. "I wrote him off."

---

6. Adapted from the Good Sense course description. Used by permission.
7. Adapted from the Good Sense course description. Used by permission.

Then a member of a follow-up mentoring group, whose mother knew James, told Jesse about James's work subsequent to the course. As soon as James finished the Good Sense course, he took his course manual to his church and started teaching the entire congregation what he had learned about biblical stewardship. When the congregation completed the course, he went to the countryside and started teaching courses there. The reason Jesse had been unable to reach him: he was on the other side of Nicaragua teaching a stewardship course!

In the political and economic turmoil that began in April 2018, the students found themselves better prepared to weather the crisis. "We have heard many times that people feel God prepared them for the crisis by leading them to this course," said Jesse. He cited the family of a woman named Shirley as an example. Before the course and the crisis, Shirley and her family had been deep in debt. While taking the course, they sold their cars and began a savings account. Following the political crisis, Shirley's husband lost his job—but they have been able to survive. "They are not living extravagantly, but Shirley feels at peace with their situation," said Jesse. "This family's experience has been a repeated theme among course graduates: they feel God prepared them for the crisis by leading them to this course."

Students Confirm Finance Course Impact

After completing the *Buen Sentido* (Good Sense) course, several Nicaraguans testified to its impact on their thinking and their lives. Here's what they said:

- Larry Mendoza said he made two discoveries. "First is the understanding that everything we own belongs to God. And second is discovering how I've been spending so much time and resources on myself when God is challenging me to think about my neighbors and to love them."
- Meylin Gaitan also described two discoveries: "The first is understanding how we live within the pull of our culture. And the second is when to earn, give, save, owe, and spend." As she counted off the list on her fingers, she smiled broadly. Standing next to her, Meylin's husband, Moises Guido, smiled with her.
- Mario Amador said he realized this: "My wife and I were spending money incorrectly with no plan or budget."

Course teacher Jesse Rodriguez summarized the course teaching this way: "As Christians we are called to be stewards of all that God gives us. This includes the money that we earn. In a world that pulls us toward consumerism and a myth that money can buy happiness, it is the responsibility of the church to respond to these myths by teaching Godly values and stewardship of our finances."

Early in 2019, the Kingdom Finance program became part of the Church Strengthening Department. With crucial help from his wife Jari and from Freddy Méndez, Jesse taught the course both to church leaders in this program and to other Nicaraguans with an interest and a need.

The Quadruple Bottom Line and the Three Mandates
By Renita Reed

The Spiritual bottom line can be viewed through the Great Commission. We all know about the great commission from Matthew 28: *[19]Therefore go and make disciples of all nations, baptizing them in the name of the Father and of the Son and of the Holy Spirit, [20] and teaching them to obey everything I have commanded you.* We are **to be disciples** and **to make disciples**. We love to ask pastors how many commands are in this text? Most say four: go, make disciples, baptize, and teach. But the real answer is only one: Make Disciples. "Go" can be explained as "as you go about your business"; and baptizing and teaching is what we do once we have made the disciples. How can we be a disciple and who can we be discipling in our place of work?

The Social bottom line can be viewed through the Great Commandment. We all know about the second great—the great commandment from Matthew 22: *'Love the Lord your God with all your heart and with all your soul and with all your mind.' [38]This is the first and greatest commandment. [39]And the second is like it: 'Love your neighbor as yourself.'* Who are our neighbors in the workplace? Customers, employees/employers, suppliers, competitors, colleagues, as well as the community where our place of work is located. How can I love them?

The Economic and Environmental bottom line can be viewed through the Creation mandate, which we (at Discipling Marketplace Leaders) are calling the Great Commitment. This comes from Genesis 1:28: *God blessed them and said to them, "Be fruitful and increase in number; fill the earth and subdue it. Rule over the fish in the sea and the birds in the sky and over every living creature that moves on the ground."* This is the first mandate that God gives—the work that man was given to do before the fall. Often we have been taught that being fruitful and increasing in number refers only to procreation or having children, but it also refers to the taking of the resources of creation, being creative with them, and then multiplying those creations so that more people can benefit from them. That is what most of us have been made to do. But we need to be fruitful and multiply within the limits God has given us, so that we are stewards and caretakers (and not simply users) of the earth.[1]

---

1. http://reedsinthewind.blogspot.com/2016/07/the-three-great-mandates.html. Renita credits Dr. Phillip Walker with helping her fit her concept of the quadruple bottom line (spiritual, social, economic, and environmental bottom lines) into the more common language of the mandates given by God in the Bible. Reprinted with permission.

Chinandega church friendship pastors with Pastor Ryan Faber of Faith CRC, Pella

06

Building Friendships Across Continents

During its first decade, the Nehemiah Center had chosen León and Chinandega in Nicaragua's Western Corridor for its work. In 1999, following the devastation of Hurricane Mitch, that area had significant needs. Few nongovernmental organizations (NGOs) were working there. Funding for the Western Corridor programs was readily provided by the center's international collaborators.[1] The work focused especially on training and counseling pastoral couples—about fifteen of them.

Some of these couples' churches completed the Healthy Churches courses of the Nehemiah Center, as well as courses which included church administration skills, marital counseling skills, prevention of domestic abuse, and HIV treatment and prevention.

In 2011, as the Nehemiah Center was wondering what a next step would look like for these churches, Joel Huyser, then Central America team leader for CRWM, conceived of an idea: church partnerships in which they could continue their own growth and at the same time be instrumental in transforming sister churches in the United States and Canada. Originally Joel named this program "Women at the Well" and envisioned its focus as assisting women and children—two groups of people most at risk in Nicaragua.

As the program developed, this original purpose broadened to include entire congregations, but the structure of the program has remained the same. It includes mutual visits, mutual prayer, and ongoing communication. The congregations commit to a minimum of a five-year relationship. A team from the church in the United States or Canada travels to Nicaragua each year. And one time in that five years, a team or person from the Nicaraguan church travels to the United States or Canada.

---

1. International collaborators at the time were Caribbean Ministries Association, Christian Reformed World Missions (now Resonate Global Mission), Christian Reformed World Relief Committee (now World Renew), Food for the Hungry, Global CHE Enterprises, Missionary Ventures International, Partners Worldwide, and Worldwide Christian Schools (now EduDeo and Tent Schools International).

64 To Be Reborn

Adrianna Herrera, a partner missionary with Resonate Global Mission, was appointed coordinator of these friendships. As the program evolved, four goals developed:
1. Cultivate healthy rhythms and practices of prayer, rest, and fellowship within the congregations.
2. Promote fellowship among churches, especially among pastors, at both local and global levels.
3. Promote teamwork and collaboration on congregational and community projects.
4. Care for the hearts of pastors and churches.

To qualify for a cross-cultural church friendship, congregations needed to complete the Nehemiah Center's Healthy Churches program. Adrianna observed, "The Nicaraguan churches need to be mature enough to see the friendship as a source of mutual transformation—not just a way to secure funding." One of the current rules for these church friendships is that the United States and Canadian churches do not provide funding for the Nicaraguan churches for the first three years of a friendship.

Pastors from Chinandega visit Pella, Iowa.

As Adrianna got to know these congregations, she recognized the extent of their development. She said, "Most of the pastors who went through this intense training are now leaders in their denominations and have dynamic churches. The Nehemiah Center invested huge amounts of time in a limited number of people and are still reaping an abundant harvest from that."

Three friendships across continents have developed: Chinandega-Pella, Acahualinca (Managua)-Oskaloosa, and León-Hamilton.

Chinandega-Pella Friendship

The Chinandega-Pella (Iowa) church friendship program began in 2011 between five churches in Chinandega and Faith Christian Reformed Church in Pella, Iowa. Teams from Pella began to visit Chinandega each year to assist with local ministries and outreach. Relationships began to develop not only across continents, but also among Chinandega pastors.

Church Friendships: Entering a Covenant

When churches enter a church friendship, the Nehemiah Center and the churches (both in Nicaragua and in North America) sign a covenant.

The Nehemiah Center commits to do the following:
- Facilitate the relationship between the North American church and the Nicaraguan churches
- Coordinate learning opportunities for the North American and Nicaraguan churches
- Promote and facilitate regular communication among the Nehemiah Center, the North American churches, and the Nicaraguan churches
- Organize and facilitate visits between the Nicaraguan and North American churches, including providing staff assistance and oversight
- Promote teamwork among the Nehemiah Center, Nicaraguan churches, and the North American church
- Appropriately manage all funds provided for the Church Friendship program and any extraordinary activities for the participating churches
- Be in regular prayer for the North American church and the Nicaraguan churches

The US and Canadian churches in the relationship commit to do the following:
- Be in regular prayer for their friendship churches, as well as sharing joys and concerns with them
- Learn from, and with, their friendship churches through training sessions, orientations, and spaces for dialogue which include regular meetings with the friendship churches and the program facilitator
- Engage in regular communication with the Nehemiah Center and the Nicaraguan churches through regular meetings and whichever media platform works best (email, Facebook, Skype, etc.)
- Visit the Nicaraguan churches at least every 12–18 months and do what is in their power to receive visits from Nicaraguan representatives to cultivate unity among the congregations, pastors, and leaders
- Collaborate on community projects or joint events with the friendship churches and/or the Nehemiah Center
- Financially support the Nehemiah Center each year, with the funds being used to support the Church Friendship program and other Church Strengthening programs. A minimum of US$3,000 is requested from North American churches, and US$50 from Nicaraguan churches.

Churches interested in exploring the possibility of a North American–Nicaraguan church friendship can email info@centronehemias.net.

"The five Chinandega pastors were already good at working together, but they were not yet friends," said Adrianna. "Over time, the monthly meetings have become times of personal refreshment for them." After participating in a spiritual retreat, the pastoral families from Chinandega decided that they wanted to do more things together.

One catalyst for deepening that friendship was a 2018 ten-day trip to Pella by the Nicaraguan pastors. They participated in Faith Church activities, helped with the church's crafts-for-

> **Transformation Story:** A Goal of Being Useful
> *Antonio Maldonado*
>
>
>
> As a child, Antonio Maldonado dreamed of studying in the United States, but that dream went dormant when he saw no path to achieve it. In 2011, while Antonio was still in grade school, people from Pella, Iowa, began visiting *Iglesia Amor Viviente* (Living Love Church) in Chinandega where his parents, Porfirio and Suyapa, were pastors. He watched the teams from afar, not interacting very much with them.
>
> In high school, Antonio began studying English because he thought it would be a valuable skill for life in Nicaragua. He began practicing his English when the teams visited. And he began to understand the teams' purpose. "I knew they were doing God's work, helping other countries," he said. What he didn't know was that God was preparing a future for him.
>
> Then the visitors told him about a chance to study in Pella for a semester. "They asked me, 'Do you want to study in the United States?'" He realized his childhood dream could become a reality. He accepted that opportunity to study at Pella Christian High School.
>
> He said, "After a semester in Pella, I heard God calling me to serve in His kingdom as a missionary." In hearing that call, he was following in his parents' footsteps. As pastors of Living Love Church, they were missionaries who had been sent from Honduras to Nicaragua in 2002. Antonio said the teams who came from Faith Church, Pella, to Chinandega had helped him see God's purpose in his life.
>
> He chose to study at Pella Christian High for an additional year to improve his English skills, and then was accepted by Dordt College (now Dordt University). Church members and other Pella area residents helped Antonio with paperwork, scholarship funding, and emotional and logistical support.
>
> In the spring of 2019, Antonio completed his first year at Dordt University where he studied engineering, played in a campus worship band, and still had a goal of becoming a missionary. "After college I want to use my knowledge to serve society," he said. "My main goal in life is being helpful for others."

sale projects, attended sporting events, and toured local industries and social service agencies.

They returned to Nicaragua with new ideas and insights. Martha Quiroz, who co-pastors *Iglesia de Dios Central* (Central Church of God) with her husband Adolfo, said she appreciated the US citizens' organizational skills and attention to detail. Paulino Muñoz of *Iglesia de Nazareno* (Church of the Nazarene) noted a different form of evangelism. "We do it more strongly with campaigns and direct preaching," he said. "I thought Pella did not have evangelizing, but now I realize that their witness is more through testimony and social work."

Chinandega pastors visit Pella, Iowa, and participate in church potluck.

They also returned with a stronger internal bond among the five churches. Pastor Porfirio Maldonado said that now he could tell the *Amor Viviente* (Living Love) denomination that there were other friendly churches in Chinandega. "Before we said it, but now we do it," he said. His wife, Suyapa, added, "The church does not look at other churches as rivals but as friends." After the Living Love denomination transferred the Maldonados back to their home country of Honduras, the other four pastoral couples made a trip there to spend time with them.

The pastoral couples are not the only people from Chinandega to spend time in Iowa. Antonio Maldonado, son of Porfirio and Suyapa, came to Pella Christian High School for a semester. His semester was funded by the Pella church's Friends of Chinandega team. That semester was followed by a full year—and then extended into attendance at Dordt College (now Dordt University). Marlo Van Klompenburg, who organized many of the Pella-to-Chinandega team trips, commented, "Antonio's presence helped to provide a cross-cultural exposure for Pella students and their parents beyond the membership of Faith Church." To enable Antonio to attend Dordt College, area residents formed a scholarship board and assisted with his college tuition.

Marlo said, "These developments were gratifying. Antonio was in grade school when we first met him in Chinandega. We saw him become proficient in English and then become confident enough to take the risk of entering another culture."

León-Hamilton Friendship

The León-Hamilton friendship was also launched in 2011, between three León congregations and Immanuel Christian Reformed Church in Hamilton, Ontario—a congregation with about 350 members with a strong Dutch ethnic heritage.

In 2004 Steve McKnight traveled to Nicaragua to visit a Nehemiah Center missionary whose work in Nicaragua was supported by the Immanuel congregation. When he returned home, his wife, Agnes, observed, "I think you left a part of your heart in Nicaragua!"

She was right, and when the opportunity for a church friendship arose, Steve was part of the congregation's outreach team that gave birth to the friendship with the three León churches: *Iglesia Belén* (Bethlehem Church), *Iglesia Getsemaní* (Gethsemane Church), and *Iglesia Monte Horeb* (Mount Horeb Church). Since 2011, Immanuel Church has sent teams to León five times.

On one of the early visits, pastors from León talked about their vision for the future. "We learned that they wanted a friendship, not a partnership," said Steve. "They were clear that they did not want the financial support and oversight that the word 'partnership' implied for them." They had been hurt when a North American church had abruptly walked away from a partnership, perhaps because its members were weary of continuing to provide financial support. They wanted a relationship of spending time together and sharing ideas. During a 2016 trip, the León

---

Transformation Story: We Worship the Same God
Larry and Kathy Groenenboom

After a half-dozen trips from Pella, Iowa, to Nicaragua, Larry and Kathy Groenenboom still have clear memories of their first visit. They especially remember a pastoral couple from Santa Matilde. "I remember how much the pastor's face shone while he told us about his miraculous healing after a motorcycle accident," said Kathy.

Larry added, "And I remember that his wife was so excited to be eating in a restaurant with the team that she called her mother on a cell phone."

But what struck them the most was how the couple beamed when they talked about God and His church.

Their hearts were touched on subsequent trips, too—by working with children in a Compassion program at *Iglesia de Dios Central Chinandega* (Central Church of God, Chinandega) and by the faith of that congregation to launch the program for several hundred children, although at that point they had found sponsors for just a handful of the children.

Over the years, Kathy bonded especially with one member of that congregation, Lorenza

Arbizu. The wall above the Groenenbooms' back door is decorated with gifts from Lorenza. "Every year she sought me out," said Kathy. "It amazed me how she fed hundreds of Compassion children from one tiny church kitchen." One year Lorenza asked Kathy to pray for her granddaughter's upcoming heart surgery—and then Kathy mourned with her when that granddaughter died. Later Kathy's grandson needed the same surgery, and Lorenza prayed for him.

During the Groenenbooms' first Nicaragua trip, Larry, who is more comfortable working with his hands than talking with strangers, stayed at the Nehemiah Center to help with building projects while Kathy went with other team members to Chinandega. He ticked off a list of the wiring and plumbing projects he completed that year.

The second year, wanting to spend more time with Kathy, he decided to try visiting Chinandega. The evening he arrived, he was apprehensive. He asked fellow team members, "As a sixty-year-old, what will I do with a bunch of kids who speak Spanish?" The next day, aided by Nicaraguan teachers and translators, he helped children make picture frames and paper baskets. He said "*Hola* (Hello)," shook hands, smiled, patted shoulders, and helped with outdoor games. At the end of the afternoon, with the help of a translator, he told the gathered crowd of children, "When I came here, I had eight grandkids. Now I think I have about fifty!" Despite his misgivings, he had enjoyed the day. Every visit since then, he has chosen to go with Kathy to Chinandega instead of working at the Nehemiah Center.

He said he's learned that kids are kids wherever you are. He added, "Nicaraguans worship the same God we do. Their style is different, but it is still the same God."

Kathy added, "I've learned that owning stuff doesn't bring contentment; relationships are important. I have a lot more friends now, and I am more empathetic with different nationalities. I don't get upset about people at the United States border. Maybe those immigrants need to cross that border!"

pastors hosted the team members in their homes. "It was a wonderful bonding experience," said Steve. "On Saturday evening we shared stories and pictures, laughed, told jokes—things that friends do together."

The bond among the three León pastoral couples has also been strengthened. "They remark again and again that they used to have no local pastor friends," said Adrianna. "Though their meetings are scheduled for two hours, often they run for three. When the Hamilton church visits, the pastors spend time with them—and with each other—discussing how they do things such as fasting, church governance, and baptism—and why they do them. They have a deep heart-level connection." She said that because the pastors value the friendship so much, involving their congregations sometimes takes a back seat.

Denis Cienfuegos, pastor of Bethlehem Church in León, observed, "We have a friendship that is very strong and special and beautiful. We have learned how to walk together and also to discover the will of God for our city, our families, and our ministries. I feel free to share what I am going through and problems in my family and to ask for prayer from León and from Canada."

His León congregation was surprised to hear about the meals that members of Immanuel took to a woman who had fallen and broken a leg. They discovered that the Canadian church takes care of its members, and they were inspired to start a weekly offering for a family with a medical crisis.

Agnes McKnight of Immanuel CRC, Hamilton, spends time with church friendship members in León.

Adrianna observed, "Nicaraguans are learning that people in other countries also struggle with broken family relationships, difficult economic circumstances, and poor health. As they pray for each other, these churches are learning to love each other more fully despite the distance that divides them."

Steve said the friendship has resulted in his congregation placing a higher value on prayer. "When someone is sick, they pray, fully expecting that God will respond. And if the outcome is not healing, somehow they are okay with that." Steve himself experienced this change when waiting for the results of testing for prostate cancer. "I was dreading the outcome. And I thought, I have all these people in León and Hamilton praying for me, and I know, regardless of the outcome, that God will be with me." When the test confirmed cancer, he was given the grace to accept that diagnosis.

Another change in the Hamilton congregation has been to place a higher value on establishing communal bonds. "We saw how the León congregations work at building community—visiting a local jail and going to the homes of people who are sick or homebound." To build stronger bonds, Immanuel Church launched Faith Families—dividing the congregation into small groups which meet one to four times each month.

One ongoing challenge for the Hamilton church, as well as the Pella church, is generating enthusiasm among members who have not traveled to Nicaragua. The outreach teams in the congregations continue to look for ways to involve more members of the congregation in the relationship.

Acahualinca-Oskaloosa Friendship

A third church friendship—between Central Reformed Church, Oskaloosa, Iowa, and three Managua churches in the Acahualinca area from three different denominations—began in 2016. By then, the experiences of the previous two friendships had shown that a relationship with three Nicaraguan churches, each from a different denomination, was probably the ideal ratio. During their visits, Pella teams felt stretched trying to spend time with all five Chinandega churches—but once the relation-

Pastor Mike Sereg and Pastor Andy Baker pray over church members in Acahualinca, Managua, Nicaragua.

ships had been established, they did not want to abandon the relationship with any of the five congregations. From the León friendship, which had two churches from the same denomination, Adrianna discovered that it is hard for the two churches that share a denomination to resist talking about denominational issues, leaving the third church outside of the conversation.

The seed for a church friendship had been planted at Oskaloosa Central Reformed Church already in 2013 when a self-study revealed a congregational weakness in global missions. They sponsored a dozen missionaries, but the majority of members could not name even one of them. There was no real connection with their missionaries. The congregation assigned Jennifer Van Zante, missions coordinator, and Pastor Andy Baker to find ways to create stronger awareness of missions.

Attending a conference, Jennifer and Andy learned about the Christian Reformed denomination's pioneering work in creating global church friendships. Then they took a fifteen-session missions course, Perspectives on the World Christian Movement,[2] recommended to them by their denomination, the Reformed Church in America. Jennifer subsequently contacted Resonate Global Mission to learn more about the Christian Reformed denomination's church friendship program. She was directed to Joel Huyser—who was going to be in the Oskaloosa area in just two weeks. "We took it as a sign from God—a way we could go deeper with one particular mission," said Andy Baker. Joel told them about the Nicaraguan church friendship program. They requested a church friendship—and then they waited for six months. Andy said, "Suddenly we received an email: 'Here are your three churches and here are the details'—and we were off!"

---

2. https://www.perspectives.org.

Meet the Team: Falling in Love Across Cultures
Adrianna and Raúl Herrera

Adrianna (Oudman) Herrera first came to Nicaragua in 2008 as part of a three-week study-abroad option at Dordt College (now Dordt University). Six years later, after finishing college and earning a master's degree in linguistics and exegesis, she returned to Nicaragua as a Nehemiah Center Cohort of Missioners volunteer. Her first assignment was helping host Church Friendship teams from North America. She soon decided to stay, and she became a partner missionary for Resonate Global Mission. She eventually became coordinator of the Church Friendship program.

A lover of languages, Adrianna was already fluent in Spanish when she volunteered in Nicaragua. At age eight, vacationing in the Netherlands with her parents, she had envied the Dutch children she met. Why? "Because they were already studying five languages in school, and the only language at my school was English." As a sophomore in high school she could finally study a language: Spanish. She studied it throughout high school and then at Dordt College—reading all of her college Spanish homework aloud in order to increase her oral fluency. She also worshiped at a Spanish-language church, where she ran PowerPoint projections for worship. After worship, she often spent time at the home of a family from Mexico, speaking Spanish with them.

Adrianna said her decision to become a missionary in a different culture was a natural step after taking advantage of cross-cultural opportunities as she grew up.

During Adrianna's first few years of coordinating Church Friendships, she lived in León with the other Cohort volunteers to work with a community development program. León was also the home city for three Nicaraguan churches in a friendship with a church in Hamilton, Ontario. And León was just half an hour from Chinandega, where five churches had formed a relationship with a congregation in Pella, Iowa.

By 2017, though, Adrianna was making three trips a week to Managua for Nehemiah Center responsibilities and other activities, and she began living in Managua instead. "The reason for living in León vanished when I was only sleeping there—and spending my days in Managua," she said. That move turned out to be crucial during the 2018 sociopolitical crisis. "León was such a political hotspot that all North American missionaries based there were evacuated," Adrianna said. "Some Nicaraguans also fled, using their tourist visas to get to North America. Living in Managua, I was able to stay in the country. If I had been living in León, I would have been evacuated."

When Adrianna first arrived in Nicaragua, someone suggested to Raúl Herrera that he date her. He said he ran the other way. The reason? He didn't speak any English, and he thought she didn't speak Spanish.

Then, when he first heard her speaking Spanish, he chuckled. "She spoke it so slowly and precisely." He obtained her phone number. They texted, dated a little, and Adrianna concluded they were not a match. Besides, she had been told it was not a good idea to start dating during her first year in Nicaragua. As she dated other men, however, she found herself comparing them to Raúl—and they didn't measure up.

Adrianna and Raúl remained friends, and eventually resumed dating in 2016. This time love blossomed, and in December 2018, they married. When they married, Raúl had already been studying English for a year. He had given up his job as a security guard to do that. Why? Because he wanted to be able to talk with Adrianna's family. "Now it is her turn to smile about my slow and careful pronunciation," he said.

In 2018 Raúl began to work alongside Adrianna coordinating Church Friendships. Adrianna and Raúl have found they have complementary skill sets. Adrianna likes the computer work, and Raúl enjoys the phone calls, scheduling, and purchasing. "He is able to negotiate better prices than I am," said Adrianna.

Each of them appreciates the other's culture. "In Nicaragua, I have learned to extend more grace to people," Adrianna said. "When I was first here, I had all the idealism of a recent college grad. I have learned that life and missions are a lot more complicated than I expected. Extending grace—even in a marriage—is crucial."

Raúl said he appreciates the equality of North American culture. "In Nicaragua, it is more important how many degrees you have and whether you earn a lot of money," he said. "North Americans have accepted me for who I am as a person."

When Central Reformed had initially inquired, the work of the Nehemiah Center was focused on Estelí, but no Estelí churches seemed like the right fit and fulfilled the requirements for entering a friendship with a US church. In addition, the center was in the midst of transferring its focus to Managua. Then Pastor Henry Cruz, who coordinated the Healthy Churches Program, suggested that Central Reformed Church might consider a friendship with three Managua churches in the Acahualinca neighborhood, including his own congregation. These three congregations had ended a partnership with a California church and were therefore accustomed to partnering with a US congregation.

When a team from Central Reformed traveled to Nicaragua in April 2016, team members discovered that they shared with the Managua churches a concern for people in poverty. "Oskaloosa is a small town with big-city problems like Managua's—drugs, homelessness, and so on," Andy explained.

Already when the friendship began, the church leadership made a concerted effort to involve the entire congregation. Key church leaders were members of the early teams sent to

Nicaragua. Then church leaders found ways to connect Central Reformed ministries—vacation Bible school, Sunday school, and its young-married group. They incorporated videos from Nicaragua into corporate worship, and dedicated a space in the church foyer to photos and information about the friendship. "We did everything we could to make the Nicaraguan churches real for our congregation," said Andy.

How has the friendship impacted Central Reformed Church? Members now are more connected to how God is moving and working in other countries; some of them have traveled to Nicaragua. Sunday-school children have exchanged greeting cards. Both the Sunday school and vacation Bible school programs have designated their offerings for the Acahualinca churches. Members have videotaped their testimonies to become part of a marriage conference in Nicaragua. Youth group members have also videotaped testimonies.

Andy said the relationship has improved his congregation's spirit of prayer. "Nicaraguan churches are passionate about prayer, and this has seeped into Central's prayer life also," he said. He also senses a more relaxed attitude in the congregation. "We were very concerned about perfection—in music, for example," he said. "Our Nicaraguan friends simply 'make a joyful noise,' and it is OK."

One dramatic result was the decision by Andy and his wife Andrea to move to Nicaragua with their family and work there. Andrea began teaching at Nicaragua Christian Academy International, and Andy worked with the Church Strengthening Program of the Nehemiah Center.

Mike Sereg, the pastor who replaced Andy at Central Reformed Church, said, "The churches in Nicaragua fully rely on God for help—not just for people but for the churches' existence. They pray with abandon, seeking God for counsel and direction. The American church at times relies on itself. We fail to ask the Holy Spirit for direction because we simply 'just do it.' Nicaraguans pray about everything, and we could learn a great deal from them about asking Jesus for help."

Working together, the pastors of the three Managua churches created a work plan in 2017 with activities to address the needs of the pastoral families, the local church, and the community. Each pastor specified material and human resources that their church would contribute to each activity. Although not all the churches had a large youth group, they decided to each invite twenty young people to a Saturday morning activity. Over sixty youth from the Acahualinca neighborhood came to play games, hear a message about God's will for their lives, watch a video testimony from youth in Oskaloosa, and eat lunch together. They left saying goodbye to new friends from other churches.

In 2018, Pastor Henry Cruz traveled from Managua to Oskaloosa. There he preached, visited nursing homes, and toured an area factory with many Hispanic immigrant employees to whom Central Reformed had been reaching out. The church friendship has increased the congregation's energy for this ministry.

In 2019 the relationship was still very young, and its focus was projects and teamwork. "All of the churches are committed to the relationship, but they are still learning how to trust each other and avoid cultural pitfalls," said Adrianna. A friendship among the three Nicaraguan pastors had not yet developed. In addition, the 2018 political crisis required energy that would otherwise have gone into developing the relationship. A further blow to the friendship was the death of Pastor Henry in April 2019, since the other pastors looked to him as the leader. They are now trying to find their way in the midst of difficult leadership circumstances for all four churches.

North American and Nicaraguan church friendship participants play dominoes together.

Transformation Stories: North Americans Comment on Trips' Impact on Them

After trips to Nicaragua in 2018, members of Central Reformed Church, Oskaloosa, Iowa, and Bethel Christian Reformed Church, Listowel, Ontario, made the following comments about how their trip had changed them.

- "Going on a mission trip to create relationship was hard for me in the beginning. I . . . have always built or worked on something. . . . Meeting with the pastors changed my heart. . . . The Holy Spirit put compassion in my heart."
  -Pastor Mike Sereg, Central Reformed Church
- "I went as a spy but came back as an ambassador."
  -Steve Vogel, Bethel Christian Reformed Church
- "Before the trip, I felt apprehensive, unsure if God was leading us to partner further with the Nehemiah Center, but now I feel assured of God's leading in this venture."
  -Bill Hiemstra, Bethel Christian Reformed Church
- "Before the trip, the Nehemiah Center felt far away, but now it feels personal."
  -Corné Koerson, Bethel Christian Reformed Church
- "It's been a longer process, but in the past I saw missions as simpler; now I realize the complexity, that there is no instant change, that results take time and a life-long relationship."
  -Henry Meinen, Bethel Christian Reformed Church

All three friendships have resulted in cross-cultural bridges: the congregations see ways in which they are different and ways in which they are similar. As they learn from each other, they are slowly transformed. "Friendship is a very apt word for these relationships, as compared to 'brotherhood' or 'partnership,'" said Adrianna. "In friendships there is freedom for ups and downs. You can lose touch for a time and then get it back." She said the Nehemiah Center is a needed bridge in helping form these friendships, but its eventual goal is to step out of that role in each relationship—and focus on launching new ones for other congregations.[3]

---

3. Congregations wishing to explore the possibility of a church friendship can email info@centronehemias.net.

In Memoriam: Pastor Henry Cruz
Former Church Strengthening Program Coordinator
December 11, 1966–April 5, 2019

Henry Cruz, a Managua pastor and teacher, joined the staff of the Nehemiah Center in 2008 to help create its new Healthy Churches program. He facilitated roundtable discussions to shape the program, and then he became its church trainer for the next ten years. He balanced this teaching role with pastoring *Monte Sion* (Mount Zion) Foursquare Church, a congregation in the Acahualinca neighborhood of Managua.

"Henry did a great job of cultivating his own church in a healthy and holistic way," said Andy Baker, a colleague of Henry's in the Church Friendship program. "He truly believed that the local church was a light to the world. He sought out every possible opportunity to mentor and train pastors, whether it was for the Nehemiah Center, his denomination, or simply other churches he knew." Andy estimated that hundreds of Nicaraguan churches have been strengthened by Henry's teaching.

Henry grew up in Acahualinca and fell in love with his future wife, Pilar, who also lived there. When Pilar's family moved out of the neighborhood, he continued to court her, traveling an hour each way by bus in order to spend time with her. They married in 1982 and subsequently had four children. As those children married and had kids themselves, they all continued to live in the Cruz home. With each marriage, Henry and Pilar added a room to their home so the couple—and eventually their children—could have a room of their own. The clan grew to include four spouses and six grandchildren, who affectionately called their grandfather "Papa Henry."

Historically, Acahualinca has been one of Managua's most financially vulnerable neighborhoods. Many residents have made their living recycling materials from the adjacent city dump. To fund church programs and building projects, Henry moved to San Francisco, California, on several occasions to pastor a Spanish-speaking congregation there. He saved his earnings for his Nicaragua church and added to those savings by cooking and selling food on weekends. When the Acahualinca church building was finally complete, he said, "That is enough," and thereafter pastored only in Managua.

He did travel to the United States again in 2018, where he spent time in Iowa with members of Central Reformed Church in Oskaloosa, Iowa, which had a friendship with Mount Zion and two other Acahualinca churches.

Henry was a skilled presenter. He was a certified trainer for both the Timothy Leadership Training Institute and *Red de Multiplicación* (Multiplication Network). His style was lecturing, using PowerPoint slides to tick off the bullet points of his presentation. "He was the most organized person I have ever met," said Adrianna Herrera, who collaborated with him when his congregation became one of the churches in the Church Friendship program. "He was organized for a purpose, in order to get a job done."

When the Nehemiah Center sponsored a workshop on love languages for Nehemiah Center staff, they discovered Henry's love language was gifts. "Shoes, cologne, food . . . it didn't matter," said Adrianna. "Henry felt valued through giving and receiving gifts."

Whenever Henry received training for new presentations, he shared that information with his own congregation, as well as many other congregations. "Until he was dying, I never knew Pastor Henry to turn down a request to do training," said Adrianna.

Late in 2018, he began losing weight and energy, which puzzled his doctors. He was diagnosed with advanced liver cancer shortly before he died on April 5, 2019.

In 2017 Henry's congregation had launched Houses of Hope, home-based Bible studies with a purpose of evangelistic outreach. Henry had set a goal of launching 150 Houses of Hope. When he died, fifteen Houses of Hope had begun. His wife, children, and church elders have begun filling Henry's roles and continuing his legacy—including his goal of launching 150 Houses of Hope.

An IMPACT Club member learns life lessons and biblical principles through participating in IMPACT Club meetings.

07

Shifting to Urban Development

In its first decade, the Nehemiah Center's community development work focused on rural areas. In its second ten years, the center shifted that focus to urban areas, with good reason: there was a dramatic global shift toward urban living. Latin America (along with Asia and Africa) was experiencing rapid urban growth.

In addition, urban centers had impact and influence on surrounding areas. According to the book *Incarnational Training Framework*, "To know our cities is to know ourselves, and what it means to be human. Cities reveal us at our best and worst."[1]

The Nehemiah Center's strategy became working with churches so they could be agents of change in their cities.[2] In the center's second decade, the need for training churches in holistic ministry—ministry to neighborhoods and communities—became apparent. From 2001 to 2014 the number of Nicaraguans professing to be Christians nearly doubled. Church buildings also multiplied. More than 95 percent of Nicaraguans professed a belief in God.[3] But the neighborhoods of those Christians and their churches continued to decline. Domestic violence, divorce, teen pregnancies, minor crimes, and youth suicides increased.

"When we started this focus, development work in urban settings was brand-new," said Alicia Hamming Navarrete, communications coordinator for the Nehemiah Center. "There were not many resources on urban transformation."

---

1. A handbook published by Street Psalms and used by the Nehemiah Center as a training guide. Kris Rocke and Joel Van Dyke, *Incarnational Training Framework: A Training Guide for Developing Incarnational Leaders Engaged in City Transformation* (Street Psalms Press, 2017), 20. Used by permission.
2. Core values of the Nehemiah Center include the Centrality of the Church and Holistic Mission. https://www.nehemiahcenter.net/core-values.
3. https://www.nehemiahcenter.net/about-us.

Strategy for Urban Transformation

In 2010 the Nehemiah Center was completing its work developing healthy churches in León and Chinandega. A logical next step for these churches was to work on building healthier communities in their surroundings. However, transitioning from rural to urban development training proved difficult for the Nehemiah Center staff person leading that effort. A replacement was needed—and found: Roberto Armas, who lived in León and had already developed relationships with the communities through his work with groups of at-risk youth in those cities. And strong relationships are crucial to transformation. Asked what program can transform lives, Bill Milliken, whose life's work has been keeping high-risk urban youth in school, answered, "I've been doing this for fifty years. I've never seen a program transform a life. The only thing that can transform life is a relationship."[4]

Under Roberto, *Estrategia de Transformación Urbana* (ETU—Strategy for Urban Transformation) began implementation in those two cities, with training provided by World Renew, a Nehemiah Center international partner. Mark Vanderwees, who worked for World Renew in Nicaragua until June 2019, explained ETU: "Urban settings often have the needed resources, but something is blocking them from being used. You need to figure out what the block is—and train people to be catalysts for change in their own communities."

World Renew's acronym for development work was ABCD: Asset-Based Community Development. Using ABCD, Roberto helps communities identify what they want, what resources they have, and how to achieve their goals. The first step for a community developer is to work with community members, identifying strengths. Relationships can grow when the developer looks closely at the community, beginning to see it as they see it. Together they come to recognize the strengths of local individuals and of the collective community. And everyone understands that community members will be closely involved in whatever plan of action is developed.

Roberto Armas (right), Community Development Program Coordinator, with Strategy for Urban Transformation community leader Danilo Blanco

Roberto explained, "This ministry is unique because it promotes using resources and potential that the community already has. Furthermore, it is

---
4. Rocke and Van Dyke, *Incarnational*, 45. Used by permission.

a program that incorporates Christian values and seeks transformation from a biblical perspective."

Roberto said, "There are many projects that come into a neighborhood but don't promote Christian values. We say, 'We can't give you a roof, but you can live in peace. You are dignified.' I believe that is key. We offer development that promotes life in people who are in the midst of much darkness."

The Nehemiah Center's vision has been for the local church to walk hand in hand with the

---

Meet the Team: Biologist Turned Community Developer
Roberto Armas, Community Development Program Coordinator

In 2007, at age twenty-seven, Roberto Armas took two important steps: he married, and he started to work for the Nehemiah Center. A trained biologist and the son of farmers, he had worked to create a refuge for sea turtles at San Juan del Sur, and he had volunteered as a student pastor. He also had taken a Nehemiah Center course for youth leaders. When the funding for his work as a biological scientist dried up, he applied for a part-time Nehemiah Center opening working with youth. When he accepted the position, he thought he would continue looking for other work in his field. Twelve years later, he was still working for the center, now full-time.

Why did he stay? Roberto said, "I like the sense of community that is fostered here. We think of each other as family. I am fascinated by the Nehemiah Center structure—we are all at the same level. Here you learn to be like Jesus, to live the gospel in a more influential way."

During his years at the center, he added a bachelor's degree in theology to his resume. Since 2014, he has also pastored a church in Telica—a town just thirty-two kilometers from his home in León.

In his community development work, Roberto helps churches make action plans together with community leaders whom the churches had previously ignored because these leaders were not Christians. He observed, "We have seen changes in twenty-one churches who have worked to become a gospel people, not only of proclamation but also of action."

Roberto grew up on a farm and outdoor work is still close to his heart. He said, "I do not like to spend time in the office working at a desk. I love being part of the projects that the church does in the community." Asked what motivates him, he said, "Doing work that contributes to changing people's lives."

Roberto and his wife, Griselda, have two children.

Meet the Team: Champion for Trauma Healing and Peaceful Fellowship Training
Mark Vanderwees, World Renew Country Consultant for Nicaragua

Following the 2018 sociopolitical crisis in Nicaragua, the Nehemiah Center's program plans had to be abandoned. When the turmoil subsided, World Renew's Country Consultant Mark Vanderwees recommended the Nehemiah Center begin workshops in trauma healing and conflict resolution.

"We weren't so sure about the idea," said Adrianna Herrera, Nicaraguan missionary for Resonate Global Mission. "Mark really had to be a bulldog, repeatedly suggesting that we begin this kind of training." Eventually Mark prevailed, and the programs subsequently met with widespread acclaim.

Mark had seen the success of the American Bible Society's trauma healing work in other countries where World Renew worked with traumatized people. That curriculum was complete and easy to use. The conflict resolution training, however, took a bit of piecing together—using some already-existing resources and creating other resources from scratch.

When the country crisis came, Mark had been in Nicaragua for sixteen years—working with five local partner organizations, including the Nehemiah Center. Long-term relationships had been important to Mark's work. "Over the years, we have learned to trust each other and do things on each other's behalf, sometimes without even consulting," he said. Over those sixteen years, Mark worked to make the local organizations more sustainable and the programs more relevant to the needs of Nicaraguans.

In developing the programs, Mark used World Renew's Results-Based Management principles. "This process gives you a framework. You identify activities and results in the short term, medium term, and long term. You look for indicators at every stage," explained Mark. "The opposite of that is to do training without measurement or following up."

Much of Mark's development work in Nicaragua has been in agriculture, the subject he studied as a college student. Already after a short-term mission trip as a college student, Mark had known he eventually wanted to work abroad. He had shifted his studies from veterinary science to international agriculture.

But he had also wanted practical business experience before launching into international work, so he had become co-owner of a Canadian feed company. After a few years he decided to begin work for World Renew. That decision was not easy. "It was a family business—I had bought into it with my brother," he said. But he felt God calling him to international work with World Renew. "I knew the longer I waited, the harder it would be to leave."

> So in 1991, after three years in business, Mark sold his ownership in the company to his brother and moved to Haiti with his wife, Nancy. The first of their five children was born there the following year. In 2003 he and his family moved to Nicaragua.
> In 2019, Mark made another difficult decision: to leave Nicaragua and return to Canada for family reasons and to use his global skills in that setting.

community for the common good, seeking holistic, participative ministry.

To begin his work, Roberto surveyed churches and communities interested in developing a leadership team. He taught these leaders in a series of workshops on community development: Asset-Based Community Development, Restorative Justice, Group Savings Banks, etc. He then worked alongside these trained leaders.

Roberto commented on the differences between urban and rural work: "Rural areas have more of a sense of community, even though they live farther apart. In urban settings each family fights for itself and is not interested in what happens to its neighbors. There is actually less communication. We work to eradicate this disunity, teaching people within communities that they need each other. This work is very difficult and requires a lot of time."

Roberto listed five principles for urban development:
1. People discover their own potential.
2. They discover they have resources that can be used to improve their communities.
3. They realize their talents and abilities are part of those resources.
4. They develop networks with others working for community improvement.
5. Communities become aware of their own histories. They become able to map their assets and resources. They create a timeline for development, and they evaluate and measure their progress.

Creating a culture of saving money is often part of the process. As a result of ETU work, neighborhoods established savings groups, whose members set aside some earnings each month.

Roberto helped seven groups in Chinandega and León create urban strategies for transforming their *barrios* (neighborhoods). Three of these groups achieved independence and were able to continue without Roberto's assistance. "They became able to develop their own plans," said Roberto. "They had a map of their resources and had the connections they needed to manage their progress."

In the León neighborhood of Eugenio Perez, the majority of families survived by foraging in the adjacent neighborhood dump. In addition to enduring poverty, the neighborhood was expe-

> **Partnering Across Continents: A Team Effort**
>
> When a León neighborhood learned about a team coming from Faith Christian Reformed Church in Minneapolis, Minnesota, to convert some strips alongside their road from dirt to cement, the Nicaraguans disagreed about the process. Alex, a León volunteer, said, "The guys said they will help get the street ready, but they want a snack to be provided."
>
> Another community member retorted, "There is no money for snacks! This project is for the good of our own community!"
>
> Brows furrowed, and voices grew loud. Roberto Armas, the Nehemiah Center coordinator, stepped in. He explained that the team from Minnesota wanted to come alongside the community in something it already wanted and planned to do. "We all need to do our part," he explained.
>
> Roberto and the leaders decided to have a town hall meeting to tell neighbors that the visitors wanted to build relationships with the community and help them on a project. They explained that the team was providing only the materials, so community members should work voluntarily. They explained the project and process to all who would be involved.
>
> The community response was overwhelming. Instead of the discord and reticence the leaders had expected, many people started preparing the street for leveling and filling in the dirt patches for the upcoming project. They started long before the deadline, and on the day of the project, everyone collaborated with the Minnesotans. Within a day, they finished filling in the curb areas that used to be dirt.
>
> The visiting team also participated in an open-air church service in the neighborhood, helped run a children's activity in the afternoon, and spent time reflecting on their partnership with the community.
>
> However, the best parts of the visit, according to both the visitors and the hosts, were the house visits in which team members listened to and prayed for community members. People who don't normally open their homes eagerly invited the groups in to pray for them.
>
> The team had a lot of stakeholders and people involved: World Renew in Grand Rapids and Nicaragua, the Nehemiah Center administration, a church partnerships facilitator, a community development coordinator, a church from Minnesota, and a neighborhood in León. Out of the struggles, in the four days of the team's visit, God brought forth something beautiful: unity amid diversity.[1]
>
> ---
> 1. Adapted from an article originally written by Adrianna Herrera.

riencing violence. "The time that has been invested with the Strategy for Urban Transformation (ETU) has not been in vain," said Ligia Berrios, who has been part of the ETU team for many years. "I have seen how this neighborhood has gone from being a dangerous place to a safe one. Now women who return home from work at night can arrive safely to their homes without the fear of being assaulted in the streets."

Part of that change came through working with community youth, who changed from being sources of the violence to being collaborators in improving the neighborhood.

Although the teams found stories of positive changes in the neighborhoods, measurable progress was sparse. World Renew considers measurable results to be crucial for continuing a program.

Then, in April 2018, the ETU programs were tabled because of the Nicaraguan political crisis. World Renew had planned a reevaluation of the Nehemiah Center's urban program but canceled it following the crisis.

IMPACT Club leader training led by coordinator Nereyda Andino

When the crisis subsided, the Nehemiah Center's energies and resources shifted to trauma healing and peaceful fellowship programs. The communities that had achieved ETU independence also participated in these new workshops.

IMPACT Clubs

Out of the Nehemiah Center's plan for community development also rose IMPACT Clubs.[5] These clubs are formed to rescue high-risk youth in need of God's love and presence. The goal: that they become agents of change in their communities as youth, rather than waiting until they are adults. IMPACT Clubs meet three or four times per month, studying a curriculum about morals, values, and relationships.

In 2013, Nehemiah Center staff attended an IMPACT Club workshop in nearby Honduras, observing club members' development in character, abilities, and social skills. While still at this training, the Nehemiah Center staff created an action plan for launching five Nicaraguan IMPACT Clubs before the end of that fiscal year. Adrianna Herrera was the first coordinator for IMPACT Clubs, and in 2016 she passed that role on to Nereyda Andino. Nereyda launched IMPACT Clubs

---

5. IMPACT Clubs were started in Romania by New Horizons Foundation, a partner of Resonate Global Mission. Seeing the clubs' effectiveness, Resonate began launching clubs in Central America as well, first in Honduras and then in Nicaragua.

with the youth in five neighborhoods of León and Chinandega, the same cities in which Roberto was fostering urban transformation. By mid-2019 there were seven second-stage, independent IMPACT Clubs and seven first-stage clubs, still coordinated by the Nehemiah Center.

The clubs have resulted in transformed lives. In León three young women had rebelled against their families and had either left home or had deeply resented their parents for past hurts. Over a six-month period of participating in IMPACT Clubs, they processed their hurts with Nereyda. They were able to give and receive forgiveness and return home. The oldest of the three was only fourteen years old.

IMPACT Club leaders donate bags full of basic goods for those in need in their community.

Also in León, a twenty-six-year-old gang member was addicted to drugs. IMPACT Club leaders invited him to their meetings. After a year of attending, he left the gang, stopped using alcohol and drugs, and started attending worship services.

In Chinandega, one group of students had very poor grades. After two years in an IMPACT Club, they improved their grades significantly. In the same city, the parents of one twelve-year-old indulged her every whim and bought her anything she wanted. She didn't value these gifts and destroyed her possessions because she knew they would be replaced. When she looked at those with fewer possessions, she felt superior and often humiliated them. Through IMPACT Club meetings and service projects, she saw the needs of less prosperous people around her. She began to appreciate what her parents provided. She wept over her insensitive behavior and realized her need to value what she had and to share it with others.

Before opening an IMPACT Club, Nereyda interviews a church's leaders to determine the congregation's level of interest. Do they have youth leaders willing to work in their surrounding communities? If there is sufficient interest, she organizes a vision conference for interested churches, presenting the IMPACT Club strategy. Churches who want to begin clubs then send youth leaders to the Nehemiah Center's IMPACT Club training.

Meet the Team: Strengthened by a Dream
Nereyda Andino, IMPACT Club Coordinator

In 2013 Nereyda Andino was president of her church's youth group when the Nehemiah Center invited her to a training in neighboring Honduras. There she learned about the IMPACT Club program. She remembered, "I fell in love with the strategy, and I knew that it was a really great way to serve God." She wanted to start a club in her church, *Santidad de Jehova* (Holiness of God) in León.

"I had a really strong feeling inside that I wanted to work with at-risk youth—those who were addicted and rebellious, who had dropped out of school, and who were unemployed." She led that youth club for two years, while she studied to become a medical technologist and also commuted to the Nehemiah Center workshops in Managua. But these multiple roles brought overload. She decided to close her IMPACT Club.

However, as she continued working at her Managua medical technologist job with a good salary, she felt empty. Something was missing. Then a fellow passenger on the León-to-Managua bus told her perhaps she needed to go back to serving God's purpose in ministry. As they continued to talk, she learned he was a pastor.

"The emptiness at work grew bigger," she said. "I told my mother and siblings, 'I plan to serve God.'" But she didn't know what that service might be.

Then she met Adrianna Herrera and learned about training to become an IMPACT Club coordinator. "I told my family I was leaving my job. My mother was upset because I had worked so hard to get a good job." For six months, her family continued to disapprove of her decision.

But Nereyda was encouraged by a dream. "I dreamed that an angel of God told me to proclaim God's Word and serve Him alone." Strengthened by that dream, she said to her family, "This is what God has told me to do."

After her training, she began working with four IMPACT Clubs in León and Chinandega as an assistant to Adrianna. Over the next two years she gradually took over more responsibility for the IMPACT Clubs, until in 2017 she became the sole facilitator for the clubs.

Her salary as a facilitator is significantly lower than her medical technology income. She said, "I may not have a large salary, but I am happy in the work I do."

In 2019, while continuing to facilitate IMPACT Clubs, she was also back in college—this time studying social work. Nereyda is married and has a daughter, Janeris Keitlin.

Once trained, these leaders select three or four church youth, and together they call on homes through the neighborhood. They especially visit homes of young people who are not yet members of a church and who are at risk, knowing the homes in which these youth live. Each month Nereyda visits the new clubs and also meets with club leaders. Four times each year she meets with the church pastors and leaders for feedback on the club's progress.

After completing the basic curriculum, each IMPACT Club raises funds for service projects by sponsoring excursions or selling food. In Chinandega one club constructed an outdoor stove near a school so that the food provided for students could be cooked on campus and students

Transformation Story: No Longer Glued to Her Cell Phone

Estefani Zamora

Sixteen-year-old Estefani Zamora lived with her parents and older brother in Eugenio Perez, a León neighborhood. She joined an IMPACT Club because she wanted help getting along with her parents. That relationship was fraught with conflict, and sometimes they just stopped talking.

What was most difficult for Estefani when she joined an IMPACT Club? Giving up her reliance on her cell phone. "For almost twenty-four hours a day I was glued to my phone. Right there, almost directly, is where the fights with my parents started because I would always be on my phone. I hardly wanted to study."

In club meetings she learned new ways of interacting and getting along. She started telling her parents what was happening in her life.

She said, "Before, I felt an emptiness—like nobody loved me. I had many problems. When you find something, such as a positive path, it changes you. Before joining an IMPACT Club, I thought my parents told me things because they didn't love me, and I felt sad. It's different now."

She is no longer glued to her phone. She surprised her parents with grade reports of 98 and 100 instead of 60 and 40. She found a friend who shared her new values. "Now my parents trust me more, and I trust them more, too."

Her IMPACT Club also began working in the local community. They gave away packages of food and clothing for children, along with games. They constructed a roof to cover a well so that people had shade when they came for water. They also painted the windows of a church.

could be fed. Previously, the government-issue food had been sent to homes for cooking, and families had consumed the food themselves rather than feeding the students.

In another project, a club partnered with Colgate in improving the dental hygiene of two hundred children. A local dentist demonstrated proper tooth brushing, and then each child was sent home with a dental hygiene kit.

In one neighborhood, club members provided an opportunity for baths, haircuts, and shaves for twenty homeless alcoholics. Club members also requested local recovering alcoholics to share their stories with these men. Four of the twenty men experienced conversions, and a former pastor recommitted his life to the Lord.

"I see God doing many things through IMPACT Clubs," said Nereyda. "Most of all, I love to see the transformation in the lives and souls of these youth. Club members become more responsible, more sympathetic, and more obedient. They love to serve and look for different ways to serve their communities. They develop more closeness and unity within their own families."

Trauma Healing Circle participants leave their pain with Jesus at the cross as part of the healing process.

08
The Nehemiah Center Responds to the 2018 Crisis

Following the suspension of programs during the 2018 crisis, Nehemiah Center staff members knew that resuming previous programs would not provide for the current needs of the Nicaraguan people.

"During the 2018 national crisis, many Nicaraguan people experienced trauma, and they had few resources to deal with it," said Andy Baker, a North American missionary working with the Nehemiah Center's Church Strengthening Program. "People had lost businesses, they had lost their security and safety, and they went to bed at night not knowing what the next day might bring."

"God challenged the Nehemiah Center to respond to the crisis in new ways," said Director Hultner Estrada. "We were called to offer pastoral companionship and comfort to a wounded society, to heal people's hearts. Amid rapid changes, we felt God walking hand in hand with us, making our path straight so that we could honor His name. He used the Nehemiah Center to bring comfort and hope, inspired by His love and His Word."

In an environment of conflict and polarization, at the recommendation of World Renew's Mark Vanderwees, the Nehemiah Center launched a pilot program of *Convivencia Pacífica* (Peaceful Fellowship) workshops and *Sanar las Heridas del Corazón* (Trauma Healing) sessions. "I couldn't be prouder of the Nehemiah Center's flexibility," said Andy Baker. "They wanted to be part of the solution as effectively and rapidly as possible. In any context, it is a big deal to totally change what you are doing. The new workshops and healing sessions are really meeting a need."

Beginning to Heal Trauma

The Nehemiah Center worked to provide needed resources with a trauma healing program created by the Summer Institute for Linguistics (SIL) and currently led by the American Bible Society (ABS).[1] The Trauma Healing Institute at American Bible Society now manages and stewards the program model and materials. Thousands of pastors, counselors, and traumatized people around the globe have used it to promote healing following trauma.

According to THI, people can be traumatized by a direct experience, by witnessing another's suffering, or even by hearing of someone's trauma. Traumatized people want to turn away from their pain, but they cannot forget it and are often unable or afraid to speak of it. Disruption of sleep, health, emotions, and relationships follows. They lose hope for the future and face a crisis of faith.

Dr. Diane Langberg, co-chair of the ABS Trauma Healing Advisory Council, says that trauma is often overwhelming. She notes four typical traits of trauma:
- Trauma overwhelms normal human coping.
- Trauma is difficult to put into words.
- Trauma shatters dignity.
- Trauma destroys ability to recognize available choices.

Questions covered in the THI trauma healing course are:
- If God loves us, why do we suffer?
- What happens when someone is grieving?

---

[1]. http://traumahealinginstitute.org. SIL authors for the program are Margaret Hill, Harriet Hill, Richard Bagge, and Pat Miersma. Used by permission.

Trauma Healing: Jennifer's Story

Sometimes during trauma healing workshops, old traumas—long untouched and unhealed—surface. This was true of Jennifer, a worship leader for her congregation.

In a small group with two other women, she thought about her childhood and burst into tears. She said, "I still had a big wound that had never truly healed. I shared with my group that the wound that affects me the most is that I grew up without a mother or father. I did not have love from them, and the family I lived with was not very loving."

She said this lack of love led to not being able to show love, and it affected all of her relationships. "Through the trauma healing sessions, I saw that we all have different wounds in our hearts. I saw that God had been working in my life. He is the one who transforms hearts, and only He can do everything."

"I also realized that time by itself does not heal wounds. After this experience, I feel God has helped me heal from losing my parents, and also prepared me to serve others. I look forward to being able to help others in my church heal from the hurts they have experienced."

- How can we forgive others?
- How can churches minister amid various causes of trauma (domestic violence, suicide, etc.)?
- How can we live as Christians amid conflict?
- How can the wounds of our hearts be healed?

The course includes creating original laments and drawings. These activities help people to express their pain instead of internalizing it and continuing to reignite it. In many countries,

Nehemiah Center and World Renew collaborate to train Trauma Healing facilitators.

the course climaxes with an opportunity for participants to take their pain to the cross of Christ. In the Nicaraguan culture, however, Protestant Christians often see the cross as a symbol of Roman Catholicism.[2] Course leaders were sensitive to this context. Instead of emphasizing the cross, they asked participants to picture Jesus, think about His healing power, and take their traumas to Him as they pinned their pain to the cross.

The course has five sessions, which can be spaced at any desired interval. Some of the Nehemiah Center courses took place over a weekend, and others met weekly for five weeks. One group of pastors chose to meet monthly.

The healing sessions are interactive—five minutes of teaching on a question, followed by discussion, dialogue, or activity.

The workshops resulted in stories and testimonies of healing. One León family had lost a son in a motorcycle accident in 2017. During the national crisis, the parents lost their business, and the church they pastored stopped taking offerings to support them. Unable to cope with the situation, their college-student daughter was hospitalized. She came to the trauma healing workshops, shared her story, and her burden lightened. She continued coming to subsequent healing circles and was able to return to her college classes. Then, for the first time, her mother told other women about her family's grief and loss.

---

2. In a Nicaraguan context, the differences between Roman Catholicism and Evangelical Protestant churches are more significant than in North America, and the relationship between Catholics and Protestants is sometimes strained.

> **Meet the Team:** Returning to God After Wandering
> *Daniel Borge, Church Strengthening Facilitator*
>
> Daniel Borge came to the Nehemiah Center in 2019 to be part of the Church Strengthening team and to assist with Trauma Healing Circles.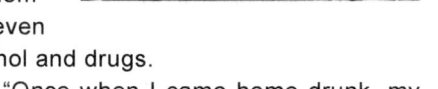
>
> Daniel had lost his previous job following the 2018 sociopolitical crisis. His employer released him when he did not sign a document or participate in political demonstrations and marches as was expected of him. He said, "Because of my faith I did not sign any documents or demonstrate, so I lost my job."
>
> Daniel was born to Christian parents and participated in church activities until he was eighteen. Later he remembered, "Then I got swept away by the world. For eleven years I was away from God." He began abusing alcohol and drugs.
>
> In that time he married and had a son. He said, "Once when I came home drunk, my son stared at my eyes and said, '*Está endrogado* (You are drugged).' That broke my heart."
>
> He went on, "I saw that I was a bad example, and I knew that only God could fill the void in me. God rescued me a second time." Since then Daniel has walked with God. He is now able to truthfully describe himself as a reliable person.
>
> In his first eight months at the Nehemiah Center, Daniel has been trained to lead Peaceful Fellowship workshops and coordinate pastoral discussions. He said, "I like to share with pastors the process of healing wounds and ways to strengthen their pastoral work."
>
> In his new role, he has had to conquer stage fright. "I used to be shy about speaking in front of people," he said. But he has been motivated by seeing the needs of churches and knowing he has the tools to help meet those needs.
>
> When he is not at work, he enjoys playing soccer with his son and daughter and spending time with his wife, Rosario Medrano.

Sometimes older, unprocessed traumas surfaced within participants. In 2016, one woman's son-in-law had killed her daughter, and then he committed suicide. This woman was left to raise her grandchildren, ages five through twelve. Andy Baker remembered, "We shared God's loving care with her. She engaged with the Scriptures and gave these burdens to God."

Some memories of trauma were far older. One participant recalled that during the Sandinista takeover in 1979, his parents fled to the United States. They left him and his siblings in the care of relatives, who locked them in a room with a bucket and let them out of that room just once per week. Thirty years later, he finally shared that painful memory.

Reflecting on the workshops, Pastor Lourdes Rivas commented, "We have been through very painful things, and [during the healing sessions] we could declare these hurts and bring them to Jesus." After carrying their traumas to Jesus, some participants were able to forgive and to reconcile with those who had inflicted their pain.

The course had a built-in multiplier effect, with selected participants invited to further training in order to become leaders for future sessions. By April 2019, the Nehemiah Center had trained thirty-three trauma healing coordinators in Nicaragua.

Learning to Live in Peace

Following the 2018 national crisis, Nicaraguan Christians not only needed healing from trauma; they also needed to learn to live together in peace. Churches had been divided before that crisis, some supporting the Sandinista (Ortega) government and some opposed to it. But after the crisis, the two sides were polarized. The divide widened into a canyon.

In response to this polarization and conflict, the Nehemiah Center launched *Convivencia Pacífica* (Peaceful Fellowship) workshops. "Peaceful Fellowship training

Trauma Healing participants share a moment of support for each other.

goes beyond processing trauma," said World Renew's Mark Vanderwees, who returned to Canada in July 2019 after sixteen years of working in Nicaragua. "At the heart of the Peaceful Fellowship program is activating what the churches can do on their own to mobilize their own resources."

Peaceful Fellowship pilot workshops were launched in León and Managua from October through December 2018. The workshops' fifty-eight participants (forty from León and eighteen from Managua) were members of churches with whom the center had worked closely on urban transformation, church strengthening, and pastoral counseling.

The Nehemiah Center chose León and Managua for the pilot programs because the sociopolitical crisis and polarization were especially evident in these cities. Family members had entered both sides of the conflicts. Some families experienced threats of violence. Others died or were imprisoned. Their relatives migrated to find safety in other countries.

Workshop participants learned about the nature of conflict and how their churches could approach it.[3] Conflict, they learned, is a situation in which a person or institution encounters opposition from another. Conflict starts with incompatible objectives which lead to confrontation.

They learned possible causes of conflict are:
- bad communication
- strong interest in the same goods or resource
- unjust structures

---

3. Curriculum for this course was created by Nehemiah Center staff using materials from the American Bible Society and Resonate Global Mission. The staff supplemented these resources with additional materials that they created themselves. Used by permission.

> **Meet the Team:** Risen from Below
> *Lourdes Rivas, Peaceful Fellowship Trainer*
>
>
>
> Lourdes Rivas has filled several roles at the Nehemiah Center over the years. Most recently she became one of the trainers for the Peaceful Fellowship seminars that were launched following the 2018 sociopolitical crisis in Nicaragua. She had previously taught courses about domestic violence and AIDS prevention.
>
> Lourdes described herself as someone who has "risen from below." In 2001, when she and her pastor husband, Alejandro, attended a Nehemiah Center healthy marriage workshop, she had not completed high school. She had low self-esteem and did not dare to voice an opinion aloud in class. Workshop leaders Luz Lopez and Manuel Largaespada treated her with respect and encouraged her to respond. Eventually, she saw her own value and potential, and not only completed high school, but also received advanced degrees in theology and psychology. She has subsequently become a leader not only at the Nehemiah Center, but also in her denomination, *Asambleas de Dios* (Assemblies of God).
>
> She started volunteering for the Nehemiah Center, and in 2007 she was asked to become part of the staff. She said, "In my twelve years of working here, I have changed my way of seeing the world—my worldview. The Nehemiah Center is interested in people in a holistic way—not just in the 'spiritual' realm, but in all areas of their lives."
>
> She added, "What motivates me here is being an important piece of the kingdom of God on earth—and helping other people in their formation. I like it that I am paid for what I enjoy doing—helping to heal hearts, listen to people, guide them, and be an emotional mentor."
>
> Lourdes and her husband, Alejandro, co-pastor *Iglesia Getsemaní* (Gethsemane Church) in León, and they have two adult daughters. Gethsemane Church is part of a church friendship program.

- differing beliefs and values
- differing or competing interests
- seeing reality in different ways
- inability to accept differences among people

They learned that conflict can go through escalating stages. It starts with tensions. These grow—leading to arguments, threats, damage, disintegration, and finally total war.

Lourdes Rivas receives Trauma Healing training to become a facilitator.

In response to conflict, people may fight, run away, or freeze. People are wired with physical, cognitive, and emotional responses to conflict. Physically, they may experience numbness, loss of appetite, or headaches. They may begin thinking in black-and-white terms and have intrusive memories. They may be irritable, cry, or experience panic attacks. They become members of a community in pain.

After learning about conflict, participants developed action plans for being a positive influence in the middle of the crisis. They were trained to create plans with SMART goals (specific, measurable, agreed-upon, reasonable, timely)—goals likely to lead to peaceful coexistence.

Old conflicts surfaced for some participants. One said, "I was divorced six months ago, after thirty-one years of marriage, and I could place myself in the village of pain. I did not see hope. I learned that I must pursue a new beginning and leave behind what cannot be resolved.... For my own well-being, I have to keep looking until my healing becomes real."

Participants concluded the course by creating their own action plans: what objectives they would pursue, where these would be realized, and how they would accomplish them.

Among the plans of the participants were the following:
- Provide baskets of food for members of the congregation most in need, asking members to give in accordance with how God has blessed them.
- Visit needy families and pray for them.
- Make visits of encouragement to families in which a parent had emigrated to find work.
- Reproduce the Peaceful Fellowship seminar for church leaders.
- Invite existing classes of youth, women, and men to participate in a conversation.

- Create a time of prayer for the nation of Nicaragua—to generate an atmosphere of trust in God.
- Offer a sewing workshop for women with limited economic resources.
- Take a prayer walk through the church building, anointing the entrances and rooms.
- Make house-to-house visits to interact with community families, carrying a message of healing and hope.
- Expand a feeding program for children.

León pastor Denis Cienfuegos said the activities were bearing fruit in his church. He said that learning to have a peaceful fellowship is producing results beyond his congregation. He worked as a counselor in a shelter for children and gave a talk to their mothers about wounds of the heart. He saw that when these women—even if they were not Christians—took their pain to the Lord, they found release.

Some participants in the 2018 pilot workshops subsequently trained as facilitators for future Peaceful Fellowship workshops, which were offered to additional congregations in 2019. Peaceful Fellowship trainers met every two months to evaluate their ongoing work.

The circles of healing which began in the 2018 pilot programs also continued to meet. Roberto Armas, one of the trainers, observed, "The program has had a great impact on participants. It has created circles of friends, circles of trust, where they can express and share the pain that is strong within them. Participants can use these circles to share and to liberate themselves from the burdens they have been feeling."

As the Peaceful Fellowship workshops continued, the Nehemiah Center's staff began to see a need for follow-up programs for restorative justice and for reducing domestic violence—which has increased following the tensions of the sociopolitical crisis. The center wanted to take these needs into account as they began preparing a new three-year plan for the years 2020 to 2023.

Prayer for Resilience

Trauma healing sometimes requires that we experience that healing with our bodies. A prayer for resilience from the workshops suggests appropriate body postures to accompany the phrases of the prayer.

(Stand up straight with your arms to the side.)
"Light of life." (Raise your hands and arms above your head.)
"Help me to be flexible" (Bend your body to the left.)
". . . and resilient." (Bend your body to the right.)
"Help me face the past" (Bend your body slightly back.)
". . . and get rid of everything I do not need to carry." (Bend your body forward and shake your hands and arms.)
"Thank you, Lord, for life!" (Stand up straight with your palms together, in front of your heart.)

Joel Huyser and Dr. Israel Ortiz at the Nehemiah Center 20th anniversary celebration

09
Planning for the Future

On Saturday, November 16, 2019, the Nehemiah Center staff was all set to celebrate the center's twentieth anniversary with a morning and afternoon conference, followed by an evening banquet and gala. Staff members had hand-delivered invitations to more than three hundred people in multiple cities. Staff had also decked the Eagle Center of Nicaragua Christian Academy International with two hundred photos, festive banners, course outlines, and miscellaneous mementoes. At 9:30 a.m., with refreshments ready, white plastic chairs in rows in the auditorium, and podiums and microphones in place on the stage, staff members opened the doors a tad anxiously. Would anyone come? They had no idea how many people to expect.

No worries. Nicaraguans from Managua thronged the doors when they opened. Then buses arrived from León, Chinandega, Estelí, and even Granada—some passengers having traveled three hours to attend the event. All totaled, 313 people attended the daytime conference.

Hugs and laughter abounded as people who had not seen each other in five, ten, or fifteen years were reunited and reminisced about their roles at the Nehemiah Center. The schedule included food, praise and worship, and music by Colombian songwriter and singer Santiago Benavides. A highlight was a set of three twenty-minute speeches by Dr. Israel Ortiz, founder of the Ezra Center, a Guatemalan organization similar to the Nehemiah Center. Each of his presentations was followed by ten minutes of audience dialogue in small groups. Dr. Ortiz based his presentations on the first two chapters of Isaiah, in which the city of Jerusalem has been destroyed and the Lord promises to transform swords into plowshares—apt passages following Nicaragua's 2018 political upheaval.

Dr. Ortiz wowed his audience. "I have never heard him so passionate," said Luz Lopez, who had worked with him in launching CECNIC in Nicaragua. Nicaraguans, who normally feel quite free to leave their seats, wander, and engage in quiet conversation during such an event, stayed seated—listening, leaning forward, taking notes—riveted to their seats.

At 2:30 the conference ended, and then in just two hours the Eagle Center was transformed into a banquet hall with cloth-covered tables and place settings for a smaller and more intimate gathering of two hundred partners and stakeholders in the Nehemiah Center ministry.

Pastors enjoy the 20th anniversary celebration.

Speaking at the banquet, Joel Huyser, one of the founders of the Nehemiah Center, reminisced about the question that had launched the Nehemiah Center movement: Darrell Mortensen, who worked for CRWRC,[1] had knocked on his door and asked the simple question, "Can we be friends?"

Then the center's current director, Hultner Estrada, talked about the challenges of the past year and the hope for the future. Santiago Benavides provided two sets of music, and the evening ended with former center director Daniel Boniche praying passionately for the staff of the Nehemiah Center and for their work.

Throughout the entire day, Joel Huyser was amazed by the way the Nehemiah Center movement had spread. He had been part of the center's work since it began in 1999, but found he knew only 10 to 20 percent of the people in attendance. "Complete strangers stopped me, expressing gratitude for this chance to gather and thanking me for my role in launching the center," he said. One woman gave him a copy of a document she had kept since the time he had distributed it at a 1998 seminar. She told him, "That conference changed my life, my marriage, my family, my church...."

The theme for the anniversary celebration was *Aguardando la Esperanza Bienaventurada* (Waiting in Blessed Hope). Two days later, when the staff members returned to their offices for their normal work routines, they were tired. "We were more than just tired, though," said Alicia Hamming Navarrete. "We were also excited—we were filled with hope!"

That hope, however, was based on more than a one-day anniversary celebration. The year 2019 had been a year of reevaluation and rethinking for the Nehemiah Center. The staff members had recognized the 2018 nationwide sociopolitical crisis as a crucial crossroads.

To assist in shaping the Nehemiah Center's future, the staff members had requested an Incarnational Capacity Assessment by Street Psalms. This assessment charted the institutional

---

1. Christian Reformed World Relief Committee, now renamed World Renew.

history of the Nehemiah Center. (See the chart on this page.) Its conclusion: the Nehemiah Center was following a typical institutional path. The years from 1999 to 2007, under the leadership of Joel Huyser, were a time of launching and growth. From 2007 to 2015, led by Daniel Boniche, the center was more mature and focused on implementing the vision through programs. Under Luz Lopez's leadership from 2015 to 2018, processes were streamlined and made more efficient.

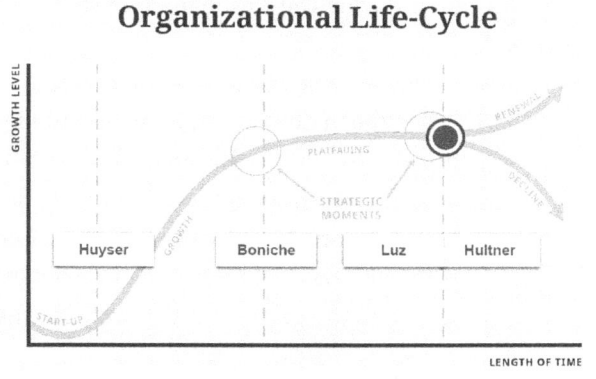

The center made the needed financial cuts. And now, as the center enters its third decade with Hultner Estrada as director, the Nehemiah Center is at a critical point in its history. It is poised for one of two futures: either decline, decay, and death—or rebirth into a different form with renewed energy.

The Street Psalms assessment helped the Nehemiah Center observe that it had shifted from considering itself to have abundance toward seeing itself as having shortage and scarcity. It also noted that during the multiple stresses of recent years, mutual trust within the center had declined.

Subsequent to the Street Psalms assessment, Resonate Global Mission sponsored a series of meetings to learn from the development of Central American interchurch relationships in both Nicaragua and El Salvador. The event was an "exercise in learning, discernment, and response" in order "to listen to God and each other, to discern where God is inviting us to join the Spirit, and to commit to faithful responses we can take together."[2] In this gathering, the Nehemiah Center and Resonate confirmed some results of the Incarnational Capacity Assessment and shed additional light on positive developments and stories of transformation in Nicaraguan churches.

Joel Huyser, who attended these meetings and now supervises all Latin American work for Resonate Global Mission, sees signs a rebirth may be in the center's future. He observed, "Although we can appreciate the Nehemiah Center's past, we don't need to be nostalgic or live under the illusion we could return to it. The current story of the Nehemiah Center is not a story

---

2. Participating in this event were Resonate Global Mission, Christian Reformed Church of North America congregations, Seeds of a New Creation from El Salvador, and the Nehemiah Center from Nicaragua.

of success or failure, but the story of the Holy Spirit's gentle work in midwifing a new birth. The stories we heard during the Resonate-sponsored meetings offered evidence a second birth is occurring."

Those stories revealed two important facts:
1. The Nehemiah Center's training provided participants with strength to face the sociopolitical crisis. At the Resonate-sponsored assessment, Pastor Gilberto Alguera testified, "The present crisis could not have been confronted without the strength gained from the past training by the Nehemiah Center."
2. The Trauma Healing Circles the Nehemiah Center started in 2018 were a just-in-time response to the needs of the church and the community in that moment in history.

By uncovering both recent and long-past traumas, the circles of healing may well be enabling people to become better agents of transformation. Richard Rohr, a Franciscan friar and spiritual writer, once observed, "If we do not transform our experience of pain, we will transmit it." Martha Cabrera, a Nicaraguan psychologist who has worked in the country for decades, maintains that Nicaragua's history of repeated sequences of trauma has resulted in a population whose trauma is unhealed. This lack of healing hinders its citizens from being energized and transformed by workshops and programs.

Nehemiah Center staff helping out and enjoying the 20th anniversary celebration

And Martha Cabrera's work reveals an underlying reason for this workshop fatigue. She found in the wake of Hurricane Mitch, when she and her social-worker team members provided opportunities for people to speak about the hurricane trauma, they also wanted to speak about earlier traumas. She said, "We found that while people wanted to talk about their immediate losses, they had an even greater need to talk about other losses they had never voiced before." [3]

When Nehemiah Center staff offered Trauma Healing Circles in 2018 and 2019, they found that same response. People not only spoke about the current trauma of the political upheaval, but also unearthed traumas long buried. Joel Huyser wonders if the Trauma Healing Circles might be

---

3. Martha Cabrera, "Living and Surviving in a Multiply Wounded Country," https://www.medico.de/download/report26/ps_cabrera_en.pdf.

a way for the Nehemiah Center to enable Nicaraguans to become agents of transformation in new and powerful ways, if the circles could be part of a rebirth.

A Professional Researcher Provides Services

Another energizing event for the Nehemiah Center as it steps forward into its third decade has been a study of the needs of Managua pastors by a professional researcher, Marisa Azmitia. Marisa had decades of professional experience gathering data for businesses. When she became a Christian, she was eager to use her skills in the service of a Christian organization.

One Sunday after worship at *Iglesia Verbo* (The Word Church), she learned about the work of the Nehemiah Center from Director Hultner Estrada, who had preached at morning worship. She volunteered her services to help the Nehemiah Center assess the needs of Managua pastors as it began to develop its five-year plan for 2020–2025. For the first time in its history, the Nehemiah Center had access to the services of a professional researcher.

Marisa's study asked pastors and leaders from thirteen Managua churches to evaluate their relationship with God, with each other, and with their surrounding communities. She compiled their responses in *Sueños Pastorales* (Pastors' Dreams), an in-depth study of Managua pastors and their congregations based on interviews and focus groups. While pastors thought their churches' relationships with God were stronger than the other two relationships, the study found they defined this relationship with God quite narrowly as prayer, fasting, and reading of the Bible. Other dimensions such as silence, contemplation, and appreciation of God's creation were not considered part of that relationship. Evidence of a relationship with God manifesting itself in interpersonal relationships, service to others, and personal satisfaction were also not a strong part of their thinking.

Relationships within congregations focused on organizational, structural, and managerial issues— on tasks, more than on meaningful friendships. This institutional focus resulted in fatigue among the pastors,

Nehemiah Center 20th anniversary conference participation

leaders, and members of the congregations. Special needs included participation of youth, cross-generational communication, and spiritual formation based on participatory dialogue rather than one-way communication.

Congregations' relationships with their surrounding communities were strong in going house to house and holding special events to evangelize, but weak in practicing the gospel by action and service in the communities. The burden for evangelism events fell to the pastors, and growth in numbers was seen as important, but growth in discipleship was not.

During a validation meeting in which pastors learned of these results, they expressed a need to receive pastoral care. They wanted a safe place outside of their own congregations where they could share their joys and griefs. They agreed they needed to pay more attention to their own physical and spiritual health.

After receiving the Pastors' Dreams report, the Nehemiah Center set to work creating its new plan. "We had been discouraged following our work with Managua churches," said Alicia Hamming Navarrete. "We did not think our work had been effective. What we discovered was a vast need, for which we had just begun to scratch the surface."

Recognizing the ongoing volatility of the sociopolitical context in Nicaragua, the planning team decided that, instead of a traditional five-year plan, they would create a three-year plan appropriate for their long-term vision and goals.

Encouraged by what they had learned through Marisa's research, the Nehemiah Center decided to create a department for research to continue gathering data-based information from Nicaraguan pastors and church leaders.

The center also decided to strengthen its programs of spiritual formation and pastoral training for Nicaraguan church leaders and to create new ones. Another strategic goal was to develop and strengthen relationships with key religious leaders through dialogue and collaboration.

In response to the Street Psalms observation that the Nehemiah Center had moved toward a sense of economic scarcity, the center decided that despite a shortage of monetary resources, it could maximize its human resources by creating a team of volunteers and increase these volunteers' capacity for useful service.

In response to a decline in trust that the Street Psalms survey had noted, the center made it a priority to strengthen its organizational and institutional life, increasing the shared vision of team members, as the center creates relationships of trust and collaboration.

Each of these goals has measurable targets for assessing progress at year-end in 2020, 2021, and 2022.

Already in 2019, the Nehemiah Center had begun several new programs which energized the Nehemiah Center's team members and participating pastors and moved toward these strategic goals. Two of these programs were Preaching Peace Tables and Replenish Retreats.

Preaching Peace Table for Pastors

The spring after the 2018 sociopolitical crisis, the center launched Preaching Peace, a roundtable gathering of Managua pastors, in partnership with Street Psalms. Twenty Managua pastors and church leaders met for discussion and personal growth, focusing on the question: how can we effectively preach peace in a time of increased polarization?

"The pastors are from varying denominations with differing theologies, but the Preaching Peace meetings became very important to them," Joel Huyser said. "They rarely missed one of the meetings."

Andy Baker, who facilitated these roundtable discussions along with two other Nehemiah Center staff, explained, "The more people rigidly entrench themselves in their opinions, the more likely conflict becomes." One pastor told Andy that he struggled to find anything to preach on that would not anger a significant part of his congregation.

Another of the pastors had a crisis on his hands after an old picture of him with a government official was posted on social media. The photo was reposted on social media, and people immediately concluded that he and his congregation were pro-government. He had to carefully explain the picture without alienating either side, a delicate balance.

Preaching Peace roundtable participants pray for their city.

The definition of peace for the group was "following God's plan for the world." The group studied Scripture passages in which God laid out His vision of peace. They also shared their best practices—examples from their preaching that moved congregants toward transformation.

When the roundtable discussions began, many of the pastors said they were experiencing high levels of stress. One pastor said that before the roundtables began, the stress had negatively affected his health. Six weeks later, his stress level had decreased, and his health had improved as he sought and shared God's peace.

In addition, nearly all participants said they had learned the importance of calling their congregations to apply the message of Scripture and the sermon in the following week.

Manuel Hernández is a pastor in the *Misión Príncipe de Paz* (Prince of Peace) church in Nejapa, located in a poor neighborhood near the Nehemiah Center. He and his wife, Rosa Argentina, participated in the Preaching Peace Table.

When asked about the impact of those meetings, he responded he practiced better personal and spiritual administration. He said, "I used to preach three hours on Sundays. I have improved to short, direct, simple preaching. . . . I treat members better. I was cultivating fear. Now I cultivate respect."

Uriel Gonzales, pastor of *Nueva Jerusalén* (New Jerusalem), a well-known church in Managua, said, "I accepted the challenge of preaching to create peace. I left the security of neutral messages, because I understood that preaching is the tool of pastors to contribute to peace in Nicaragua."

Another goal of the Preaching Peace Table was to encourage pastors to aim at transforming the lives of their congregations and to listen to people surrounded by chaos. One of the pastors in the group responded to the sessions by preaching about Jesus reaching out to the blind beggar Bartimeus, who had been rejected and reduced to begging outside the city walls. His congregation responded by inviting young drug users to their church building for a time of food, fellowship, and conversation.

When the first set of twenty pastors concluded their seven-week series of roundtable discussions, a second group of fourteen pastors began to participate in a new round of these sessions. The Nehemiah Center had not planned a second round until 2020, but participants in the first session were so enthusiastic, they invited pastor friends to join a second set of meetings. With a group already recruited, the Nehemiah Center decided to offer the roundtables again in 2019.

Replenish Retreats

Even before the April 2018 sociopolitical crisis, Nehemiah Center staff members were seeing increasing numbers of pastors with signs of burnout. As staff members discussed pastor burnout, several of them were reading the book *Replenish* by Lance Witt.[4] After the crisis, Marisa's research confirmed the high level of burnout among Nicaraguan pastors.

LiderInnova, an organization in Costa Rica, had translated and contextualized Lance Witt's

---

4. https://replenish.net/about. Used by permission.

work, creating videos and discussion materials in Spanish.[5] Eight Nehemiah Center members used Witt's work to create a pilot retreat for themselves. Personally rejuvenated by the retreat, they adapted it to the needs of Nicaraguan pastors. The first pastors to go on Replenish Retreats were pastors from León, then from Chinandega, and finally from Acahualinca. They were pastors whose churches had friendships with North American congregations.

Nehemiah Center staff adapted the retreats into five ninety-minute sessions offered over a two-day and one-night time period. Each session featured a brief overview by a facilitator, a fifteen-minute video from Lance Witt (dubbed in Spanish), a short follow-up presentation from the facilitator, fifteen minutes of large-group discussion, and thirty minutes of small-group discussion. Facilitator Andy Baker commented, "We found the small-group discussions to be especially important because they allow pastors to share their struggles with others who are in similar positions."

Pastor Pilar attends a Replenish retreat with her family.

The five retreat sessions were:
1. **Behind the Scenes:** How we connect with God in our personal life is as important, if not more important, than the actual work we do in ministry.
2. **The Gift:** We need to focus always on the gift God has given us rather than getting lost in the details of ministry.
3. **There Is a Hole in My Bucket:** Ministry can be draining. How do we fix the problem areas of our life and ensure that our bucket (soul) never runs dry?
4. **Waiting for Snow:** It is important to take time for a day of rest and connection with God.
5. **The Stake:** We make changes in order to strengthen our connection with God and establish healthy ministry habits.

The fourth session, on having a day of rest, has been especially challenging and important. Andy explained, "Pastors have come to believe taking a sabbath is not for them. If they take a

---
5. https://www.liderinnova.net. Used by permission.

sabbath, they feel their members will think they are lazy and not fulfilling their calling to the fullest. Once pastors understand the importance of a sabbath, we help them design a plan to take a sabbath. We also explain that it's important to start slow." For pastors currently working a seven-day week, the leaders suggested starting with just three hours of rest per week for three months and then gradually increasing their time for rest.

Both the Preaching Peace Tables and the Replenish Retreats have been especially promising because they are responses to data-based information about pastors' needs and they are dialogue-based: the pastors talk with the leaders and with each other and walk the roads of preaching and of renewal together.

In Summary

During the center's second decade, many changes occurred. But, as Adrianna Herrera observed, "Walking with people is a long process. The details of the Nehemiah Center's work have changed. But its heart remains the same: a belief in God's work of transformation."

In its first decade the Nehemiah Center was born out of the vision of three very different missionaries to Nicaragua in the wake of a natural disaster, Hurricane Mitch.[6] As the center ended its second decade, it faced a new disaster: social and political upheaval. Perhaps through this second disaster, it has been moving toward rebirth.

Joel Huyser characterized the November 2019 anniversary celebration as a testimony that the Nehemiah Center is not a lifeless monument, but a living movement with a hope and a future. "We do not rely on the Nehemiah Center as an institution. We work and pray for the continuing of a movement which spreads spontaneously, in which the Spirit is active, in which there is life as people influence those around them, and as all see themselves not as recipients, but as active participants. Together, we are all responsible for that future."

The challenge toward continual rebirth confronts us all, as together we wait in blessed hope, that each day, each hour, each moment, we will be reborn.

---

6. Institutional founders of the Nehemiah Center were Darryl Mortensen (CRWRC—now World Renew), Ken Ekstrom (Food for the Hungry), and Joel Huyser (CRWM—now Resonate Global Mission). They were joined by many others in their founding of the center.

Appendix A
Nehemiah Center Vision, Mission, and Identity Statement

Vision:
We see healthy churches, actively growing in holistic mission.

Mission:
We facilitate opportunities of growth and collaboration for churches and para-church organizations in order to serve them and to strengthen them in holistic mission for the advancement of the Kingdom of God, locally as well as globally.

Identity Statement:
The Nehemiah Center is a community of learning and service that contributes to the formation of leaders and the continuing training of pastors using a biblical and holistic worldview, and that cultivates local, national, and international collaboration for Christ-centered cultural transformation of communities and nations.

Appendix B
Nehemiah Center Core Values

Biblical Worldview
We see the world and all of creation through the Bible's perspective. The creation of God is good, and even though corrupted by human sin, it is being reconciled to God through Christ (Colossians 1:15–20). For this reason, the Nehemiah Center seeks the lordship of Christ in all aspects of life (Isaiah 9:6–7) and sees the church as the body of Christ, called to be His ambassador of reconciliation in the world (2 Corinthians 5:17–20).

Servant Leadership
We recognize that Jesus is our model of servant-leadership (Mark 10:45) and that He shows us how to influence the lives of people and communities with love, humility, integrity, and respect (John 20:21). We acknowledge the gifts and abilities as well as the weaknesses and needs of ourselves and others and the necessity of transformation in our lives and contexts.

Centrality of the Church
We hold that the local church is the principal agent ordained by God for the advancement of His Kingdom on earth (Acts 1:8), commissioned by Christ for the proclamation and demonstration of the Gospel (Romans 10:11–17). Each church is called to live as the incarnated body of Christ, and her members are called to live intentionally, making a difference in all spheres of life and society (Ephesians 4:11–16).

Holistic Mission
We seek the transformation of the culture of the local church, family, and professional sectors into the culture of the Kingdom of God (Romans 12:1–2) so that, together, all spheres impact the different ideologies, values, and practices of society (1 Corinthians 3:5–7) through a servant-hearted leadership.

Collaboration
We value and model the diversity and unity of the body of Christ (John 17:20–21). We encourage and cultivate spaces for mutual learning and cooperation on a local, regional, and global level for the common good and for the fulfillment of the Great Commission (Matthew 28:19–20) and the Great Commandment (Matthew 22:34–40).

Appendix C
Nehemiah Center Strategies

Contribute
Contribute to the health and growth of the Nicaraguan and Latin Church to develop holistic mission.

Cultivate
Cultivate cross-cultural relationships between Nicaragua and North America that contribute to the health and growth of the North American church to develop holistic mission.

Collaborate
Collaborate with organizations that prepare, equip, and send people into cross-cultural settings that contribute to the health, growth, and holistic mission of the global church.

Strengthen
Strengthen the capabilities and shared vision of the International Collaborators team and the institutional health of the Nehemiah Center.

Appendix D
How to Serve the Nehemiah Center

Come on a Short-Term Team (7–10 days)
Short-term teams are a great way to learn about the work of the Nehemiah Center and begin to understand the context of our ministry. Teams are invited to come spend time learning about Nicaragua, see what makes the Nehemiah Center unique, and serve in specific areas of interest such as church strengthening, education, business, and community development. Teams are facilitated through one of our International Collaborators. For more information contact info@centronehemias.net.

Be a Volunteer (2–12 months)
Come for an extended visit to Nicaragua and stay between 2 and 12 months by volunteering at the Nehemiah Center. This is a great way to connect and build relationships with Nicaraguans, really learn the culture, and improve your Spanish language skills. There are a range of volunteer opportunities available at the Nehemiah Center. For more information on specific opportunities and volunteer needs, please write us at info@centronehemias.net, including a cover letter telling us about yourself and your CV or resume.

Complete an Internship (3–12 months)
Combine education and practical experience by participating in an internship geared to your area of study at the Nehemiah Center. Options include Education, Business, Theology and Missions, Community Development, International Relations, and Communications. If you are interested in learning more about participating in an internship, please contact us at info@centronehemias.net.

Join the Cohort of Missioners (1–year program)
Spend a year in an intentional community and be transformed by your experience of immersing yourself in the Nicaraguan culture, serving alongside grassroots leaders and growing in spiritual formation. The Cohort of Missioners is for young adults looking for a break from academics to focus on creating a greater sense of self-awareness and gain practical experience. For more information on how to join the Cohort of Missioners, contact us at info@centronehemias.net.

Appendix E
How to Donate to the Nehemiah Center

US Donations
United States residents can make direct donations to the Nehemiah Center through our affiliate, Friends of the Nehemiah Center: https://www.friends-nc.org/

Canadian Donations
Canadian residents can make direct donations through our partner organization, Resonate Global Mission: https://www.resonateglobalmission.org/support/donate-now

About the Author

Carol Van Klompenburg has written articles, plays, and books, and taught nonfiction writing at two Iowa colleges. Her published titles include *Tending Beauty: Forty Moments in my Gardens* and *On Mended Wings: Transforming Lives and Communities in Nicaragua*. *To Be Reborn* is her ninth book. She lives in Pella, Iowa, and can be reached at carolvk13@gmail.com.

www.ingramcontent.com/pod-product-compliance
Lightning Source LLC
LaVergne TN
LVHW061216060426
835507LV00016B/1962